The Catholic Highlands of Scotland
Volume 2 – Primary Source Edition

Frederick Odo Blundell

By Dom. ODO BLUNDELL, O.S.B., F.S.A.Scot.

CATHOLIC HIGHLANDS OF SCOTLAND
THE CENTRAL HIGHLANDS

With Thirty-three Illustrations. Price 3s. 6d. net (postage 5d.)

CONTENTS

THE CATHOLIC HIGHLANDS OF
SCOTLAND

INVERGARRY CASTLE

[*Frontispiece*

THE
CATHOLIC HIGHLANDS
OF SCOTLAND

THE WESTERN HIGHLANDS
AND ISLANDS

BY

DOM. ODO BLUNDELL, O.S.B., F.S.A.(SCOT.)

Author of
" The Catholic Highlands of Scotland (Central Highlands)"
" Ancient Catholic Homes of Scotland "

SANDS & CO.
37 GEORGE STREET, EDINBURGH
15 KING STREET, COVENT GARDEN
1917

AUTHOR'S PREFACE

Soon after publishing the first volume of " The Catholic Highlands of Scotland," I was able to spend two months in Rome, where the archives of Propaganda were most courteously placed at my disposal. As the time was limited, I confined myself entirely to copying such letters as related to the Highland District. These copies lay untouched, until the present war, and my appointment as Catholic chaplain with the Fleet, gave me an unexpected opportunity of putting them in order. They then afforded me great interest and helped to pass the long winter evenings. But the circumstances were not altogether favourable for writing, since there were no books of reference at hand by which to check my own statements or those of the writers of the letters. This must be my apology if any inaccuracies have crept in. Once again I must thank those who most kindly read through and corrected each chapter, as also those who assisted me with the illustrations.

F. O. B.

H.M.S. *Agincourt*,
   18th July 1916.

CONTENTS

LIST OF ILLUSTRATIONS

THE CATHOLIC HIGHLANDS
OF SCOTLAND

BARRA

MENTION of Barra and its adjacent islands occurs in
the correspondence of Father Francis White and his
companions with their Superior, St Vincent of Paul.
Father Dermit Dugan had been sent, along with Father
Francis White, to the Hebrides in 1651, and laboured
there with great zeal, but unfortunately his strength
failed him, and he died in 1657, as he was about to visit
the Isle of Pabba. The following is one of his letters,
which I give almost *in extenso* :—

"LETTER of Father DERMIT DUGAN, priest of the Congregation of the Mission, Missionary Apostolic in
the Hebrides, and in the Highlands of Scotland,
to the Very Rev. F. VINCENT OF PAUL, Superior
General of the said Congregation of the Mission.

"MOST REV. AND DEAR FATHER,—If your Reverence
has not yet received any news of me, I may say that this
has not arisen from want of diligence on my part. God
knows how much fatigue and solicitude the delay has
cost me, and the enquiry after this first opportunity,
which I trust will indeed prove a safe one. The Hebrides

being very far from the mainland, and not having intercourse with the other districts, the opportunities of sending letters to distant places are very rare. To arrange some means of correspondence I have been forced, however unwillingly, to desist from the pressing duties just begun by me, for the salvation of these poor Islanders, and to return again to Scotland on foot with great fatigue in order to establish, as I have done, a correspondence with your Reverence. . . .

" Having by God's help somewhat recovered [he had fallen ill on arrival at Glengarry] I left my companion Mr Francis White in the Highlands of Scotland, whilst I went, conformably to my orders, to the Hebrides, where God has deigned to make use of me, a most unworthy instrument, to work the effects of His great mercy, having prepared for me the hearts of all these people, who welcomed me as an angel from Heaven, especially the Laird of Clanranald, Lord of the Isle of Uist, to whom His Divine Majesty gave the grace of conversion along with his wife, his son, their family and all the gentry, their vassals.

"MacNeil, Lord of the Isle of Barra, having heard of me, sent a gentleman to beg me to do his island the same service as I had done to the Laird of Clanranald. The Lord of the Isle of Capaga (*sic*), who is a nobleman of importance, together with seven or eight of the chief gentry of those parts, made me similar requests, whom I shall with God's help, satisfy as soon as possible.

"I was also occupied with the inhabitants of the Islands of Eigg, Islay and Canna, in which 800 or 900 persons have been converted. These were so little instructed in the Christian religion that there were scarce 15 of them who knew any of the mysteries of our holy Faith. I hope that others will soon follow the example of these first converts. The chief desire of these people is to acquire the knowledge of the elements of our holy Faith, and that with so great ardour, that when I am teaching Christian doctrine the noblemen and married ladies often beg me that I would question them in public to the end that—as they said—their minds might be more impressed with what they heard.

"I found amongst them persons of 70, 80, 100 and even 120 years of age, who had never received Holy Baptism; these I instructed, baptized, and after a short time they passed to a better life. At this moment, no doubt they are praying God for those who have procured them so much good.

"The greater part of the inhabitants were living in concubinage, but we have remedied this by joining in matrimony those who were willing, and separating the others. I have found some of the inhabitants of Uist, who called themselves Catholics, and had some knowledge of the Sacraments of Penance and the Holy Eucharist. This was due to their having been to Confession and Communion formerly to some Fathers of the Order of St Francis who came here from Ireland, but these people were so little instructed that they did not know how to make the sign of the Cross.

"Money is very scarce in these parts; nevertheless everything is very dear here, and what increases my poverty is that I need two men; one assists me on my journeys and in passing from one island to the other, and when I travel by land he helps me to carry the vestments for Mass and my few other effects, I myself having quite sufficient difficulty in walking on foot over bad roads as much as 14 or 15 miles before saying Mass. The other attendant, whom I have instructed to that end, assists me to teach the Pater, Ave, and Credo, and serves Mass, there not being any one else except him who can do so.

"The want of means wherewith to purchase a small boat for crossing from one island to the other has prevented me from making more journeys; for although we are in great need, still we have not received anything from these people, amongst whom (as some are very timid) the contrary practice would have hindered the fruits of our labours not a little. . . . Ordinarily we take only one meal a day, which for the most part consists of nothing else but barley bread or oatcake, with cheese or salt butter, and we pass sometimes whole days without being able to find anything but what we have carried with us. Our drink in summer is plain water, and in winter we have a little meal boiled in it, which indeed is very injurious to my health, being as your Rev. knows, of a phlegmatic temperament. It is true that in some places we find a little beer or whisky, but this is of rare occurrence. Any one who wishes to have meat must buy a whole beast, a stirk or an ox, because there are no butchers in this country.

"The meat which the Islanders do sometimes eat, makes one disgusted, for they are content to half cook it on the embers, and then they throw it on the ground on the straw, which with them serves for table, table cloth and plate, so that we scarcely ever eat it. (Note I.)

" When we travel in summer, it is necessary to make in the forest some sort of hut in which to pass the night, or else to sleep in the open air on the ground, exposed to the weather, against which we protect ourselves as best we can, with our cloaks which we use in this country in place of the ' ferraiola ' ; but even when we reach some cottage, we often do not find any straw to lie on.

" In these Islands and in the whole of the Highlands of Scotland there are no priests except my companions and myself ; but in the Lowlands and the Eastern district, where English is spoken, there are between Regulars and Seculars six or seven in all, who are reaping great fruit, especially the two sent by the Congregation of Propaganda.

" Since God opens with so great generosity the treasures of His mercy for the conversion of these people, I think that the greatest service your Rev. can do them, is to despatch persons who are able to instruct them, who know the language of the country well, and especially who know how to suffer hunger and thirst and to sleep on the ground. It is further necessary that we have an annual salary, otherwise there is no means of our subsisting. We would also need a schoolmaster to teach the youths, and he too must have his salary. . . . I write nothing to your Rev. of the good success which God gives to the labours of Francis White, my companion, whom I left on the mainland, as I hope he himself will give an account of it."

Throughout these accounts of the early missionary labours in the Highlands and Islands, when it is said that so many persons were " converted," this must be understood of their being granted the grace of the sacraments which hitherto they had never had any opportunity of receiving; and of acquiring correct instruction, in place of the erroneous ideas which the absence of proper teachers had allowed to grow up amongst them. This is clearly proved by the following extract :—" The natives of the islands adjacent to Scotland can, as a rule, be properly called neither Catholics nor heretics. They abhor heresy by nature, but they listen to the preachers· from necessity. They go wrong in matters of faith through ignorance, caused by the want of priests to instruct them in their religion."

For the same reason many had not received baptism, since we know from other sources that those who wished to remain Catholics had the greatest objection to being baptized, and to having their children baptized, by any but the Catholic priest. No doubt this is also the reason for what is stated in the letter that many were living in concubinage—no priest had come that way to bless the marriage.

The islanders had a great devotion to holy water, and their requests for it are often mentioned at this period. In the report written a few years after the foregoing (1655) it is stated : " In the Isle of Barra there was great dearth of seaweed, which the sea ordinarily throws up upon the shore and with which the inhabitants of that island are accustomed to manure their land. Mr Dugan went to the place where they generally gathered it, and having there sprinkled Holy Water, that same day the sea threw up so great a quantity, that it lasted them the whole year."

A little further on, the same report states : " In the

aforementioned Island of Barra, a young man having been converted, along with his brothers and sisters, as well as the son of the minister, their devotion gave great edification to all the country round. All the people of that island are so anxious to learn, that when Mr Dugan had taught a little boy the Pater, Ave, and Credo, on returning to the same place two or three days later he found that all, both young and old, had learned the ·prayers. There are many other places of which the inhabitants have been converted and ask for more instruction. There are between 6,000 and 7,000 souls in these places, some of whom are far distant from others, whence it is most difficult to serve them all, unless the Missionaries who work there are assisted by others."

Father White appears frequently in the history of the mission at this time, and especially under Glengarry, where he had his chief abode, and where he died in 1679. It must suffice here to give the character of him as presented by Mr Alexander Winster, the Superior of the Mission, in his Report for 1668. He says : " Francis White, an Irishman, aged 45, studied Philosophy and Theology at St Lazarre, Paris, in the Congregation of the Mission, and was there ordained priest. In the Highlands of Scotland, where he has laboured for fifteen years, he has shown himself to be a priest most ready to undergo labours and poverty, and to be most zealous for the salvation of souls. The Highlands indeed owe him a great deal."

In the same Report the Prefect speaks of the Catholic school in Barra, and regrets that in seventeen years the schools in Glengarry and Barra had given no fit student to the Mission. He proposes to start a school in the

Enzie instead. However, in 1700, Bishop Nicolson speaks of the school in Barra, but after that date we hear no more about it.

Our next source of information is dated 1671, when Mr Francis Macdonel[1] reports : "The Isle of Barra is six miles long and three broad. The landlord is the Laird of Macneil ; there are about 1,000 Catholics in it, amongst whom is the laird himself. Father George Fanning, a Dominican, labours here with good results. This father, according to the Procurator of the Mission, has no patents or faculties from the Sacred Congregation. His ground for staying there must be either the privileges of his Order or else because he believes that these people, being as it were abandoned and in extreme necessity of Sacraments, any priest may come to their assistance. This is indeed one of the strongest arguments urged by almost all those working in these British Isles and also in England ; and they claim to have a right to continue their functions and their work, all the more as they persuade themselves that recourse to Rome is either impossible or unnecessary, and that the delays of that Court are intolerable. For these reasons they think that they should not leave those souls to perish. However, these and similar views are creeping in very fast, and if they are not remedied by giving them Superiors, very few will in time have recourse to the Holy See."

There is much more of interest in this Report, which is, accordingly, reprinted here in part.

[1] The name Macdonald appears in various forms, and frequently the name of the same person is written differently in different documents. I have endeavoured, as far as possible, to retain the spelling in the documents themselves, even at the risk of apparent inconsistency.

"Father FRANCIS MACDONEL to Monsignor BALDESCHI, Secretary of Propaganda.

"ARMAGH, 10th *July*, 1671.

" When I heard that His Grace the Primate of Ireland had received from the Sacred Congregation the care of the Scottish Islands, or Hebrides, I hastened hither to Armagh from the Isles, in order that I might suggest how the Faith might be propagated in those islands. His Grace himself greatly desired this summer to return there with me, but I was of the contrary opinion, inasmuch as a report has spread of the arrival of the French, whom the Scots are said to favour, so that if his Grace the Primate were to go there, every one would think that he had come to prepare the way for the French. It is for this same reason that no Missionaries are to be sent there this summer, as the news of their arrival would at once get abroad and they would be cast into prison. For it is proposed to effect the union of the two kingdoms of England and Scotland in one Parliament, to which union the Islesmen are strongly opposed. Now, if the Primate were to visit them, it would at once be said, that he came to foster the opposition to this union.

" The best and safest method of propagating the Catholic religion in these Islands, and of strengthening it for the future, is to select some youths and to send them to Rome, or to the seminaries on the Continent, to be educated and promoted to the priesthood. Being natives, these may later do much good in the Isles and will be more gladly welcomed there. Meantime, his Grace the Primate should send thither some Irish priests or religious, since the people of these islands understand nothing but Gaelic and they can hope for spiritual assistance from none but the Irish, since the Scots (Scoto-Angli) speak a corrupt form of English, and experience has long since proved that they afford no spiritual help to the Isles.

" Moreover, so small an allowance as fifty scudi [1] is not sufficient for the Missionaries destined for that field of labour. A priest must support, besides himself, one and perhaps two servants to carry the sacred vestments, books and other things from place to place. Now, what are fifty scudi a year amongst two or three ? Certainly were I not related to the Lords MacDonell, who have great influence in these islands, I could not have subsisted there until now. Father George Fanning also, of the Order of Friars Preachers, would have perished from hunger before now, were it not that he lived with the Laird of Barra. He has not received a sixpence from the Sacred Congregation for the past eight years, although he has laboured much and with great fruit. I myself have received nothing for two and a half years, and three years allowance will be due me next February. The Sacred Congregation only gave me one vestment, when two were very necessary, for the journey has often to be made from island to island, and there is great danger and difficulty in taking vestments between the five islands where there are Catholics. Indeed there should be one set of vestments in each island, so that the priest be saved the labour and the danger of carrying them about.

.   .   .   .

" From my receiving no answer to them, I conclude that my various letters to the Sacred Congregation have

---

[1] Five scudi were worth £1.

been lost on the way, and hence in future I shall write through His Grace the Primate, and I shall hope for the reply also through him. It would greatly help our Mission if a letter were sent to the Marquis of Antrim, who is of the family of MacDonell, and has many followers in the Isles; also it would be a good thing to write to the most noble Donald MacDonell, Chief of Clanranald, for though he externally professes to be a heretic, still he is very well disposed towards us and has a great number of Catholic dependents; lastly it would be of great service to write to the illustrious Gillerane MacNeil, of Barra, who is a Catholic."

The Report of the Archbishop is almost a repetition of the points suggested by Father Macdonel. It will be noted that the Archbishop himself reported unfavourably of the proposal to place the Scottish Hebrides under the jurisdiction of the See of Armagh, and his reasons as given below are cogent enough. Presumably nothing further was heard of the proposal, though at a later date we find Bishop Nicolson placing one Vicar-General over the Highland priests, and another over the Irish of his vicariate. With the appointment of a separate bishop for the Highlands in 1731, such a measure ceased to be of any use. After giving a list of the larger islands and their dimensions the Archbishop states:

" The proprietors of the Islands possess vast dominions on the mainland of Scotland, of which the inhabitants are much inclined towards the Catholic Faith, whereof they retain many signs and rites; whilst they dislike the Protestant ministers, even though the lairds follow that creed for political reasons.

" On this point the Procurator of the Missions has considered the advisability of NOT separating these Missions from those of the mainland of Scotland since the Lairds are able, so long as the Missions are thus united, better to protect them and to prevent discord. Besides, those gentlemen, not being able to learn distinctions of jurisdiction, desire the Missionaries, according as there is need, sometimes to go to the mainland and sometimes to the Islands, and if they were to decline to do so, they would run the risk either of being removed from the Mission, or at least deprived of protection. The fact is that the Lairds rule these people very despotically and the Missionaries must not offend them if they wish to live there.

" In the Islands wheat is not indigenous, but there is barley, oats and spelt. Oxen, cows, horses, flocks and deer abound, also fish and birds in great variety, and a great quantity of fish are caught. In these islands are no woods and no fruit trees on account of the violence of the sea winds, especially the north winds, which burn and cut up everything."

The writer goes on to describe the ordinary food, which is just as stated by Father Dugan. He also speaks of the poverty of the priests and of their hardships, and adds : " Whence one can gather that no stranger Missionaries will be found willing to come to the assistance of these people, to whose hardships they either cannot or will not accustom themselves, as experience shows only too plainly. Hence there remains but one means of helping them, and that is by schools in which youths may be taught here. For if the boys are sent away from the islands, we run the risk of their never returning any more after they have tasted the delights of Italy, France or Flanders. Indeed it will exceed our expectations if those who have been brought up there will be willing to return to teach, without the inducement of a good salary.

" The Archbishop of Armagh writes that the best method of propagating the Faith in these islands is, first, to send there Missionaries knowing the Gaelic language, well grounded in virtue, and inflamed with zeal for souls. The Procurator of the Mission, however, is of opinion that the Irish are scarcely fitted to minister there, inasmuch as there would be danger of the jealousy of the Royal Council, and if this were aroused, the liberty now enjoyed would be lost. Hence it is necessary for many very important reasons to do everything as far as possible by means of priests of their own nation, and to leave the jurisdiction over these people with those who are Scotch by nationality, and that the Irish be there as their assistants.

" Secondly to send youths of that nation to be educated in parts beyond the sea, who would be more acceptable to these people than foreigners. On this point is copied *in extenso* the reflection made thereon by the Procurator of the Mission, who says : ' You would hardly believe the affection which these people bear towards their compatriots, and the facility with which they lose that title, inasmuch as those who go away, and are educated outside their Highlands, are no longer considered such, and are called Anglo-Scotch. Hence it is most necessary that the youths be taught on the spot the knowledge necessary for Sacred Orders.' "

Regarding the statement that there are no trees in

these islands, it is noteworthy that this want has partly been supplied by Nature herself, a very large amount of timber being washed ashore on the west coast of the islands.   This is no doubt due to a great extent to the influence of the Gulf Stream, which washes ashore the timber from many a vessel which has been wrecked in the gales of the Atlantic.   For generations this was the free gift of Nature to the islanders, but not many years ago the Board of Inland Revenue declared such timber to come under their control, and it is now sold by Government.

What is said above about the jealousy of the Privy Council of Scotland as regards Irish influence is better understood when one remembers that only twenty-five years before, Montrose had, time after time, defeated the forces of the Covenant—and of the Government—by the aid of his Irish veterans, sent to him by the Marquis of Antrim, of whom mention is also made in the foregoing.

Our next source of information regarding Catholic life in Barra is the report of Mr William Leslie, written after his Visitation in 1678.   He is always entertaining, and his description of the lairds of Barra is quite in accordance with all we know of the history of that clan.   What would Propaganda have said if a case of "priest-stealing" had come before them ?   He says : " Having attended to the most important affairs of the Catholics of Canna, we embarked for the Isle of Barra.   The wind failed us and night came on, and with the night, a thick heavy fog, so that the sailors themselves lost their bearings, and we were in a pitiable plight.   I proposed that as the summer night was short they should not row, but should wait for the daylight when the sun might pierce the mist. The Skipper however pretended that he knew the course, and wanted the sailors to take to their oars. Others wanted to follow a different course, and being contradicted by the Skipper and by Munro, they threw down their oars, and putting their hands on their weapons prepared for a murderous fight. This lasted for some time. The danger was that we might pass the Islands and be carried out into the ocean, where in an open boat without a compass we might drift to America or Nova Zembla, and would all certainly be lost. What was at the bottom of the trouble was that another boat steered by the best Skipper in the country had followed another course, and now they were sorry they had not done so too.

"In the end the sailors again took to their oars and rowed on, not caring where they might land, or whether they never landed at all   With that the mist began to lift and the Island of Uist appeared close at hand. I set myself to rouse their spirits, telling them to keep the island in sight till daybreak; this they did, but they were hard put to it through hunger and the long watch, yet before sunrise we landed on a small islet and rested there some hours. About nine o'clock in the morning we landed in Uist and after having taken some refreshment we sailed to the Isle of Eriska, where we stayed eight days. We were well received and kindly entertained by an old lady, the widow of the former Laird of Moydart. Here we ministered the rites of holy religion as usual to all the Catholics, who came in crowds from far and near.

"Having engaged a boat we sailed to the island of

Barra. Here we stayed thirteen days, treated right royally in various parts of the island, but particularly by the Chief in his strong castle of Kismula.[1] This is a huge building, reared on a great rock and completely surrounded by the sea. Whatever member of the family is in possession of it, even though not the eldest, is regarded as Chief of the whole island. I visited every district, and the Sacraments were administered and all the services held for the benefit of the Catholics, who gathered round us every day with equal joy to them and to us. When we were on the point of leaving, the inhabitants showed themselves much displeased with Munro, because he would not remain with them, and if I had not been with him, I firmly believe that they would have kept him by force. Indeed they had some idea of keeping me, imagining that since I was an official of the Pope, if they retained me in their power, they could make a treaty with His Holiness to obtain priests from him as the ransom of his delegate. I had as much as I could do, even backed by the Laird, to escape from them, and then, only by promising to go to Rome and throw myself at the feet of His Holiness and put before him their neglected condition and their spiritual needs. At length after much weeping and many laments they agreed that I should depart, and Munro with me, but they swore blood-

---

[1] An interesting prophecy is connected with Castlebay. It stated that the MacNeils would be lairds of Barra until the bay was a forest of trees. The bay is nearly a mile square, and very deep in parts, so that there seemed little chance of its becoming a forest, or of the MacNeils ceasing to be lairds of Barra. However, they sold their whole property some fifty years ago. It might seem that the prophecy had failed, therefore, but that is not so. Nowadays in the fishing season the bay is so crowded with boats that a person standing on the hill which overlooks it sees nothing but the masts of the fishing fleet—a very forest of trees.

curdling oaths that if they did not get a priest of their own and Munro or any other came to the island, he would not be allowed to leave, except by swimming, as he would get no boat. They swore that they would sooner burn their boats than let another priest leave in one. Indeed it would be quite in keeping with the character of these Islanders that they would send an expedition to steal the priest of a neighbouring locality, and this would be the cause of deadly enmity between them."

Mr Leslie estimated the number of Catholics in the Highlands at 12,000, with three or four priests, all of them except one from Ireland. From other sources we know these priests to have been Fathers Francis White, George Fanning, Francis Macdonel and Robert Munro. It was largely owing to the representations of Mr Leslie that the first Vicar Apostolic for Scotland was appointed in the person of Bishop Nicolson. As has so often happened in the history of the Church, men of remarkable ability have been found for posts which appear to have been called into existence at the very moment when these men were at hand to fill them. Such a man was Bishop Thomas Nicolson, such also was Bishop James Gordon, his coadjutor and later his successor.

Bishop Nicolson's episcopate began with trouble. Consecrated in 1695 at Paris, where he was in exile, he was delayed a year and a half in Holland, waiting for a favourable opportunity of crossing to England. At last he arrived in London in November, 1696, only again to be cast into prison, where he was detained for six months. In July, 1697, he arrived in Edinburgh and undertook the duties of his office. In September of that year he wrote

B

to Propaganda : " I have not as yet been able to visit the Highlands districts, where I fear the labourers are few and the harvest abundant. . . . An attempt was lately made to establish schools in the Highlands, but less successfully than we anticipated, for the whole of that country is full of garrisons, and the missioners are not permitted to live in one place, which is greatly to our disadvantage. Experience has taught us that in certain districts of the North, where the protection of a great noble, or a less hostile attitude on the part of the people, have made it possible for priests to reside, matters go much better, for every day a certain number are reconciled to the Church."

In the year 1699 Bishop Nicolson commenced his visitation of the Highlands, and in 1700 he completed it. In his official Report, he says : " Our party arrived in Barra on the 10th of July. The island is six miles long, productive of good crops of corn, with very rich grazing. The lord of the island, who was very zealous, received the Bishop with great respect. The people, who are excellent, really deserve a good priest but we had only one of the Franciscans escaped from Ireland to place there until God should provide otherwise. In Barra there are the ruins of two or three churches and of a priory at Kilbar. There are six other inhabited islands, which belong to Barra, and there is a chapel in each. Of these Vatersay is the largest, with a circumference of five miles, while there are fourteen other smaller islands that are only used for pasturage."

Unfortunately Bishop Nicolson does not tell us the name of the Franciscan whom he left in Barra, but from Mr Thomson's list we know it to have been Mr Carolan.

As he had come to the Highland Mission in 1687, there is good reason to believe that he was in Barra all that time, since at that period the priests moved about very little from one district to another, though within their own district they were always on the move. In 1728 Father Kelly, another Franciscan, was in Barra, and as he came to the mission in 1725 this latter is probably the date of his arrival in Barra. He was certainly there in 1730, and also in 1736, when he was succeeded by Mr James Grant.

Mr Grant was still in Barra in 1746, when he was arrested and imprisoned in Inverness. After undergoing great hardships, he was liberated in May, 1747, upon condition that he would present himself when called, which he never was. The most ample testimonials were given by the minister and other Protestants of Barra, of his peaceable and inoffensive demeanour during the time of the Rising. His health had suffered severely from the hardships of his imprisonment, and he never returned to the Isles. From 1755 to 1766 he was coadjutor of the Lowland district, and in the latter year he succeeded Bishop Smith as Vicar Apostolic. He died in 1778.

For some years previous to 1762 Mr Æneas Macdonell was priest in Barra, but he died at the early age of thirty-six, in the tenth year of his priesthood, having come to the Mission in 1752. For a couple of years there was no resident priest, or, as Abbate Grant puts it, " they have been deprived of a priest since the death of Mr Æneas Macdonell, except such assistance as Diana and Tiberiop. can give them " (Bishops Hugh and John MacDonald). In 1765 Mr Alexander MacDonald was the priest of

Barra, where he remained until his election as Vicar Apostolic of the Highland District in 1779. Mr Allan Macdonell (senior) succeeded, and in 1783 his congregation numbered 1504, according to Bishop Alexander MacDonald's Report. He was soon after appointed to the Seminary, where he died, very piously, in 1788. Mr James Allan Macdonell (junior) was here for some years, and it was during the time that he was priest in Barra that there was considerable friction between himself and the laird. Bishop John Chisholm, writing in 1799, does not mention the question in dispute, but says : " Since I wrote you, I have received two letters from Mr Allan, of which one is very long and which I shall bring for your perusal. In it he gives some light relative to his innocence and Barra's persecution. Barra's conduct from first to last is of a more black complexion than I at first imagined. He is very unjust to me and to him. Mr Ranald McEachan came over to give me any information he could relative to the subject, and returns to-morrow with a worse idea of McNeill than he had when he left home." From the " Life of Bishop Hay " we learn that when the matter was taken to court in Edinburgh the Lord Advocate befriended Mr Allan and considered the complaint lodged by McNeill to be trivial.

From 1805 to 1825 Mr Angus Macdonald was in Barra. He was born in 1760 and was ordained in 1785. After his long stay in the Isles, he was sent, in 1826, to Rome, as rector of the Scots College. During his residence the Barra congregation attained to numbers which it has probably never since equalled. Bishop Ranald MacDonald states, in his Report for the year 1822, that "Mr Æneas Macdonald is in Barra. He is 60 years of age and two years ago counted 2,600 Catholics in his district, of whom 200 emigrated last year." About this date we have interesting evidence how completely Catholic Barra has always been. The Old Statistical Account of 1797 states that "St Barr is the Patron of the island and has given to it his name. The 25th Sept. is dedicated to his memory, and is observed as a holiday. On this day the priest says Mass and all those of the Romish religion used punctually to attend. After Mass the people amused themselves with horseracing and spent the evening in mirth and conviviality." Of late years this custom has been much on the decline. The same account gives eloquent testimony to the Catholicity of Barra. "The population in 1755 was 1,150, and in 1793, 1,604. The number of Protestants has always been so small that it was thought unnecessary to put the heritor to the expense of building a church. There is no manse."

Here may be fittingly inserted the testimony of Bishop John Chisholm regarding the Catholics of the Hebrides, and especially those of Barra. Writing in 1804, he says : "Many of the Catholics [of his vicariate] lead excellent lives and are most steadfast in the Faith. Some however, who live among non-Catholics or are near cities are less careful in their lives and less firm in the Faith. Those in the Western Isles and especally in the islands round Barra are splendid Catholics, who in the innocence of their lives and the firmness of their faith resemble the early Christians, and have the greatest horror of heresy."

The later priests have been Mr Neil Macdonald (1825-1835), Mr William Mackintosh (1835-1839), Mr Donald Macdonald (1839-1851), Mr Colin Macpherson (1851-1855), Mr William Macdonell (1856-1867). It was he who built the "new" chapel at Craigston, of which it was said, at the time of its opening: " It can bear a fair comparison with the best of our Highland churches." This chapel was built on the same site as the previous one, which was longer, lower and narrower. One of the oldest residents has kindly supplied me with details of the building operations at Craigston—then the only church in Barra : " All the able-bodied Catholics in the island worked and laboured in one way or another at the building, even small boys did their bit.   The boys brought cockle shells from ' Traigh Mhor ' in creels or baskets on the backs of the Barra ponies.   These shells were burned into lime.   A smack with lime and slates landed a cargo at Castlebay.   This cargo was conveyed to Craigston in the same manner.   All the heavy wood used for couples and joists was drift wood washed ashore from the Atlantic.   Stones were brought in large quantities by fishing boats from the islands of Vatersay and Sandray, and at high tide were dropped on beaches at Borve and Craigston.   They were conveyed to the building by Father Macdonell's cart and another belonging to a merchant in Castlebay, for the Crofters of Barra had no carts at this time.   Father Macdonell collected as much money as he could amongst his Congregation ; but this, I believe, did not amount to very much, as money was scarce here in those days. Father Macdonell also collected money in Glasgow and elsewhere.   I am told that the cost of the building was £700 over and above the free labour given."

After Mr William Macdonell Mr John Macdonald was priest (1867–1883), and he was succeeded by Rev. (now Canon) Chisholm (1883–1903).   Canon Chisholm built a

CASTLEBAY

The Catholic Church and Ancient Castle of the MacNeils

To face page 23

very pretty little chapel in the island of Mingulay, but in consequence of the regulations of the Congested Districts Board it is no longer used, the whole population of Mingulay having been transferred elsewhere.

Canon Chisholm's chief work, however, was building a new church at Castlebay. In 1887 he appealed as follows :—" The want of a second church in the island has been greatly felt for some time past. The present church which is seated for 500 does not give more than half the accommodation which the Congregation would require, since it numbers over 2,200 and in summer during the fishing season it is increased by at least 400 more. It is useless therefore to suppose that one priest can attend to the spiritual wants of such a large congregation widely spread as it is over a group of eight different islands, the approach to which is not only a difficult, but a very dangerous task. It is self evident therefore that the building of a new church and presbytery has now become a matter of the greatest necessity." This appeal was accompanied by a very strong recommendation from Bishop Angus Macdonald, who was always so zealous in building fresh churches, and in furthering any proposals for advancing the interests of the Catholic Church in his diocese.

Two years later an extremely pretty church was opened, and we can forgive the reverend gentleman the touch of pride when he saw his work completed, and wrote : " The church is beautiful in design, and the workmanship is substantial enough to withstand the Hebridean gales for a century or two to come. The site is extremely well chosen, resting on the crest of a rugged and steep crag, overlooking the village of Castlebay, and the historic

castle of the warlike MacNeils. It will be a landmark
for the daring fishermen of Barra, as they venture to
and from their deep-sea excursions . . . the church even
now, in its unfinished state can fairly claim to be second
to no edifice erected for divine worship from the Butt of
Lewis to the wave-worn cliffs of Barrahead."

Canon Chisholm henceforth had charge of the new
church at Castlebay, to which he later added a good
substantial house. He was succeeded in turn by Rev.
William MacMaster, Rev. Donald Martin, and Rev. Hugh
Cameron. Rev. William MacMaster had the satisfaction
of finishing the work begun by his predecessor and of ex-
tinguishing a heavy debt on the church and presbytery.

The older chapel at Craigston was attended by Rev.
Angus Macdonald (1889–1893) and Rev. William
Mackenzie (1893–1913), who in 1906 opened a third
church at North Bay, five miles from Craigston. It
is a pretty little building, and a great convenience to
the numerous congregation around it. Near by are the
hallowed ruins of old St Barr, or Kilbarr, where may be
seen the remains of the old altar, and in a recess near the
entrance the holy water stoup, bearing silent yet eloquent
witness to the unchanged faith of Barra. By the death
of Father Mackenzie, in 1914, the Highlands lost one of
their most devoted and industrious priests—one indeed
whose life had been shortened by his constant labours
and by his utter unselfishness. I well remember the last
time I met him—at the blessing of the memorial to the
late Father Allan Macdonald, of Eriskay, who had been
his lifelong friend—and two more worthy men it would
be hard to find. The morning proved so stormy that it
was with difficulty that I could get a boat to cross from

South Uist to Eriskay, whither Father Mackenzie and the rest of the clergy had gone the previous evening. When at length I managed to secure a boat, the crossing was lively enough. The piper who had come with me started his lament, the strains of which could only be heard on shore as the little boat rose on the crest of the great waves. The effect to those gathered outside the Eriskay chapel was very striking.

The storm was far too severe to permit the outside function to proceed, and though the memorial stone was blessed quietly in the afternoon there was no possibility of any of the clergy crossing to the other islands to get home. On the following day the gale still continued, but the different priests—there were seven of us—were bound to return to their respective parishes. Father Mackenzie and a young priest on holiday were seven hours in an open boat crossing home from Eriskay to Barra. They had no shelter from the wind and waves, so that on reaching their destination the younger priest had to be carried ashore in so exhausted a condition that it was many days before he recovered from the effects of the voyage. Such was but one incident in the life Father Mackenzie led, but it made me realise that though some things may have changed for the better since the days of the early missionaries, the storms of which they complained are still very severe, and the life of the priest in the Outer Hebrides is now, as ever, one of no little danger and self-sacrifice. NON NOBIS, DOMINE, NON NOBIS, SED NOMINI TUO DA GLORIAM.

SOUTH UIST

FATHER DERMIT DUGAN,[1] whose letter has been quoted at length in the preceding chapter, arrived in Scotland in 1652 and proceeded to the Hebrides, where he was received "as an angel from Heaven" by the laird and people alike. Father Dugan laboured with great zeal in this district, but his strength gave way, and he died only five years after his arrival. His death is thus described: "There still remained an island named Pabba (six miles south of Barra) which he had not visited. It was a wild and weird place. The inhabitants were not attached to any heresy, but they were totally without instruction. Father Dugan hoped to bring numbers of them to the practice of religion. He had his preparations made for setting out to Pabba on May 10th, 1657, but his strength failed him. He fell ill and died in the Island of Uist on 17th of the same month. The people amongst whom he ministered long mourned his loss; they revered him as a Saint, and gave his name to the chapel where his remains were laid to rest."

The next island to Pabba is Sandray, which I remember visiting under strange circumstances. I was staying with Rev. Hugh Cameron, then priest of Barra, when a sick call came from Sandray, asking the priest to visit that island.

---

[1] He appears in Gordon's "Catholic Church in Scotland," pp. xv. and 627, as Dermit Grey, but his own letters to Propaganda, of which several are extant, give his name as Dugan.

26

SANDRAY CROFTERS   *To face page* 27

He invited me to accompany him, so we started off together in an open sailing boat. When we reached the little bay, which is the only landing-place in the island, we had no small difficulty in scaling the cliffs to reach the row of cottages which overlooked the sea. It was an ideal October day, and the view from the cliffs out to sea was very beautiful. The cottage, where lived the old lady who was ill, was most scrupulously clean, and she herself had that air of dignity and refinement which one so often meets in the Highlands. As a child she had lived in Sandray, but her parents had been evicted, and throughout her life she longed to return to the green crops and the heather-clad slopes of the island. She had no family. A niece of hers married and went to Sandray with her. A short time previously her nephew, without asking leave of laird, factor or anyone else, had sailed across from Barra with his few sheep and other effects and had settled on the old family croft. He rebuilt the house, sowed his plot of potatoes, and was joined by two other cousins with their families. The children were the nearest approach to angels in human form that Father Cameron or I had ever seen. There were four of them—the only children on the island—and the happiness and joy of life which shone in their faces was a real pleasure to behold. How long the party of squatters were allowed to remain, I never heard, but the incident impressed itself deeply on my memory.

After Father Dugan's death, Father Francis White often crossed over to Uist. Writing in 1665, he says : I did not receive the letter of your Reverence [St Vincent of Paul] until the month of June, because my devoted friend and at present my Superior, Mr Winster, did not wish to risk it, not knowing where I might be, for since last September he had heard nothing from me. I was indeed very far from him in the Western Islands all that time, and so had no chance of writing to him."

In 1671 Father Francis Macdonell was priest in Uist, and he sent a lengthy report on the state of the Catholic religion in the Hebrides to the Archbishop of Armagh, who forwarded it to Rome.   It has been quoted at length in the preceding chapter.   Father Macdonell came to the Highlands in 1667, and was still there in 1677.   Later Father Robert Munro included Uist in his wide field of labour.   He was acting as Dean at the time of Bishop Nicolson's visit in 1700.   Of his visit to Uist the good Bishop writes : " About midday of June 23rd, which was Sunday, we landed at Loch Eynort in Uist, where Mass was said in a tent which we erected on the beach. Towards evening we went to the house of the laird at Ormaclate, and were received with many marks of kindness by his lady in the absence of the Chief of Clanranald, whom we had left on the mainland. . . . In South Uist all the people were Catholics, except about forty persons, who attend the Minister's chapel.   At twelve stations such as presented themselves were confirmed, the numbers reaching over 800.   We were greatly pleased with the kindness of the Chief of Clanranald and of his lady." Father Munro, mentioned above, had come on the mission in 1672.   In this same Report, Bishop Nicolson mentions that there were three schools in the Highlands, one in Uist, one in Barra, one in Morar in Arisaig.

The year after this Visitation we find Fathers Shiel and M'Fie in Uist, but as their names only appear in the list of clergy for that one year, we must assume that they were of the number of those priests who came from Ireland, and who in many cases could not stand the very trying conditions which prevailed in the Highlands.

The next priest who is directly connected with Uist is Mr Alexander Paterson, who was certainly there in 1728, having at that time been twelve years in the Highland Mission. Mr Paterson was still in Uist in 1733, and probably also in 1734, as in this latter year he was transferred to Strathbogie. He was succeeded by Mr Alexander Forester, a truly wonderful priest, whose record is thus told by Abbé Macpherson :

Alexander Forester entered the Scots College, Rome, in 1727, at the age of twenty-six, and left it priest in 1732. He arrived that same year on the mission, and was charged with the care of the Catholics of Uist. In 1746 he was taken prisoner, and carried up to London, where he remained, aboard a man-of-war, for six months. He thereafter was removed to Newgate Prison. At last he was banished for life, and arrived in Paris in the autumn of 1747. Here he continued till the summer of the following year, though he ardently desired to return immediately to his flock, who, he knew, stood greatly in need of his assistance ; but he could not undertake the journey for want of money to defray the expenses. After many petitions, he at last got a small sum from Propaganda for that purpose, and immediately set out. He arrived safely, and immediately took up his quarters in Uist, where he was much beloved, and where he did a vast amount of good. This excited the jealousy and spleen of the Presbyterian ministers, who accused him of plotting against Government, and of recruiting men for the French and for the Pretender. They even procured an order to bring a party of soldiers to the island with a view to apprehending him. He was well aware that should they succeed in their design, even his life might be in danger, not on account of their calumnies, which they could never prove, and which he could show to be false, but because he had returned from perpetual banishment, to which he had been condemned under pain of death. For this consideration all his friends advised him to retire. He again left his numerous flock, absconded amongst the hills, until he found an opportunity of passing over to Ireland in 1754, from whence he returned to Edinburgh almost immediately. After a few months, hearing that the soldiers had left the island, and that the Presbyterian ministers had become more remiss in their search for him, he returned to his charge, where he continued to labour with great zeal, for many years thereafter Abbé Macpherson adds: " I have not learned the date of his death." This, however, took place in December, 1780, when the venerable priest had attained the age of seventy-nine, having been forty-eight years on the Highland Mission, and almost the whole of that period in Uist.

Several notices are extant concerning the life of Mr Forester. In 1763, Abbate Grant, agent in Rome, stated in his Report that " when it was at all possible there were always two priests in Uist ; now on account of the great dearth of Missionaries they have to do with one, Mr Alexander Forester, a truly saintly man but advanced in years, being over 60. He had been an Alumnus of the Scots College, Rome."

Bishop John Macdonald, writing in 1766, states that

he himself had been stationed in Uist almost ever since he came to the Highland Mission (1755) till he was made Bishop in 1761.

In 1766 Mr Wynn had recently arrived in Uist, according to Bishop John Macdonald's letter to Propaganda, where he says: "Mr Wynn is indeed a laborious and willing man, and behaves to everybody's satisfaction, for which he shall receive all the kindness we can show him. He is settled with Mr Forester in South Uist, where he has enough to do, his companion being now old and infirm, so that the chief weight must be upon him, which he bears very cheerfully." Mr Wynn left Uist in 1770, "to our great disappointment," writes Bishop Macdonald; but the times were too difficult for him, since during his years there was begun in Uist the most remarkable persecution of the Catholics, of which there is record in modern times.

It appears that the laird of Boisdale, Alasdair Mor Macdonald, was publicly censured by the priest because he had compelled his people to work on St Michael's Day, the patron saint of the island, and celebrated by the people as a holiday of obligation. The priest ordered Boisdale out of the church, at that period a frequent penance, and one which was well understood to mean a temporary punishment. On the following Sunday persons so punished would return to church as usual, but Boisdale never returned. So far both accounts which I have received agree. The Directory of 1851, however, states that it was Mr Wynn who rebuked Boisdale, and places Mr Wynn's residence in Uist "between 1715 and 1730." Now we have Bishop Macdonald's own statement that Mr Wynn was priest in Uist between 1766 and 1770. Did this incident then really occur between these latter dates ?

Certain it is that Boisdale, who in his earlier years had been a Catholic, began about 1768 violently to persecute his former co-religionists. To such a length did he go that Bishop Macdonald and the clergy brought the miserable state of their people before Bishop Hay, who in their interest issued a public Memorial drawing attention to their sufferings. In view of the position of Bishop Hay at the time, and of the fact that the Memorial was given full publication, there can be no doubt about the truth of the statements therein contained. The Memorial is here given almost in full, only two copies of it being known to exist.

:" MEMORIAL for the suffering Catholicks in a violent persecution for religion at present carried on in one of the WESTERN ISLANDS of SCOTLAND.

" *An example unheard of in our days !*

" The Island of South Uist, one of the largest of the Western Islands of Scotland, is the property partly of Clanranald and partly of his cousin-german Macdonald of Boisdale. This last, besides what he possesses as his own property, has also very large tracts of land in lease, from his cousin Clanranald, so that he may have between 250 and 300 families of tenantry under him, all of the Roman Catholic religion as all their predecessors before them had been. Boisdale himself was baptized, and in his younger days brought up in the same Church, but is now a Protestant. About two years ago, he took the resolution to cause all the people under him to embrace the Protestant religion and to extinguish the old religion entirely as far as his power reached.

" To do this his first step was to invite all the children in the neighbourhood to learn English and writing with a Presbyterian preceptor whom he engaged in his family for the education of his own children. This the poor people, suspecting no harm, gladly agreed to, and numbers of children were sent accordingly ; but how greatly were their parents astonished, when after some time they understood that the most shocking methods had been used to corrupt their children ! That impious blasphemies had been daily inculcated into them against their religion ; that wicked, immoral and even immodest sentences had been given to be copied over by those who could write, and that when the time of Lent came, in the year 1770, flesh meat was forced into the mouths of those who refused to eat it, in contempt of the laws and practice of the Church in that holy season.

" No sooner were the parents apprised of these things, than with one accord they called their children home, and absolutely refused to allow them to frequent such a school any longer. This exasperated Boisdale to the highest degree ; he stormed and threatened to eject them out of their lands, but the poor people preferred their duty to God, and the peace of their own consciences to the fear of man, and disregarded all his threats in such a cause. Boisdale, suspecting that their pastors had encouraged them to this conduct, turned his fury against them ; forbid them ever to set foot in his lands, or exercise any of their functions amongst his people, threatened them with the last dregs of his vengeance if they acted

C

otherwise, and to treat them with indignity with his own hands wherever he should meet them. These gentlemen, for prudence sake, kept retired for a little time, where the necessity of their duty did not call them ; in the hope that a little cool reflection would mitigate his anger, and make him more moderate. But it was all in vain, he still continued fixed in his purpose, whilst the poor people, though exposed to every sort of maltreatment from him, were resolute in suffering all, rather than act against their consciences, so that not a single person yielded. At last, some time before Whit-Sunday 1770, he calls all his tenants together, and tells them, that he had taken his final resolution, and had drawn up a paper in English which he would read to them in their own language, and was determined that either they should sign the paper, or be thrown out of their holdings. He then read this paper to them, which to their utter amazement, they found to contain a solemn renunciation of their religion, and a promise under oath, never more to go near a priest.

" The poor people were shocked to hear such a proposal made to them ; but he, persisting in requiring them to agree to it, or leave his lands, they made not the slightest hesitation on the part they had to act, but to a man, renounced his service, and gave up their lands, resolved to beg their bread from door to door, rather than be guilty of such impieties. This was a step he did not expect, and which quite confounded him, for he was sensible, that if he should let them go, his lands must lie waste for want of inhabitants. Upon this, finding himself forced to yield, he called them back and offered to give them terms. The first he proposed was, that he should give them no further trouble themselves, upon account of religion, provided only they allowed their children to be brought up Protestants; to which they unanimously replied, that the souls of their children were as dear to them as their own, and that to do a thing to their children which they believed to be prejudicial to them, was involving their own souls in the same destruction.

"Upon this he seemingly complied with them, and engaged them for another year upon his lands, to give them time, as he said, to think better on it. But no sooner had he got them fixed than he began his former solicitations, and endeavoured by every means he could think of, to force them to compliance, all which they resisted with the most heroic constancy.

"Then it was that a proposal was made to them, by their friends on the mainland, to try to get them settlements in St John's Island, in America, where a gentleman of their clan was purchasing a considerable property, principally with the view of assisting them and others oppressed at home. But as the poor people for the most part were unable to transport themselves thither with the necessary provisions, utensils, etc., they were not willing all at once to leave their native country, in hopes that their master would at last relent and let them live in peace. But in this they found themselves much mistaken, for since then he has become much worse than before; for finding them determined never to renounce their religion, he has used every means in his power to reduce them to beggary, in which he has but too well succeeded; and he now tells them that they must leave his lands next Whit-Sunday, and go to America, if they please, when he knows that the greater part of them have not one farthing to carry them anywhere. The latest accounts of them are contained in a letter from Bishop Macdonald dated the 29th of last October, of which the following is an abstract :—' Since every method failed him, he betook himself to all the artful means his malice could devise, and has reduced them in their circumstances within these two years past to such a degree that few of them are worth one half of the stock they had before that time, and the greatest part of them are reduced to beggary, with their numerous offspring in a remote island, 30 leagues from the Continent, not knowing what hand to turn to, and without any means of getting out of such a goal (*sic*). Their distress is still heightened by the prospect this destructive season presents them with, whereby the generality of these countries is threatened with destruction.' Bishop Macdonald then enumerates the measures taken by Boisdale to effect his end ; 1°—by raising their rents to three- and fourfold what they formerly were ; 2°—keeping them in constant agitation, and that at the busiest time of the year, so that they were forced to neglect their crops ; 3°—perpetrating all kinds of oppression upon them, while they, being 100 miles from any Justice of the Peace, have no form of redress. He continues : ' To these oppressive measures he adds the most barbarous treatment of their persons, never accosting them but by the terms ; You devil etc. : and venting such blasphemies against every article of their religion, as makes death more eligible to them than the having any connection with him. The uncommon veneration and attachment to landlords and chieftains, for which they were remarkable, is by such barbarous treatment changed into an extreme of terror and with one accord they pray God to deliver them from him. Those who are the more immediate objects of his fury and who are under an absolute necessity of leaving him, are about thirty-six families who dwell on those lands which are his own personal property. The rest who are his subtenants upon the lands he has on lease from Clanranald, amount to about 600 souls, but with these he has not proceeded to such violent excess; and it is hoped that if he finds the former taken by the hand and provided for, he may, for fear of losing the whole, mitigate his cruelty against the rest, and give them some better terms. Now as the only way to provide for these heroic sufferers, is to get them over to St John's Island, where the above-mentioned gentleman will provide them with land on the most advantageous terms, though it is not in his power to carry them over; and as it is impossible to raise such a sum of money in their own country as would be required for their passage, provisions, and the other necessaries for a new colony, the only resource they have under God, is to recommend themselves to the charity of all well-disposed Catholics, hoping the above plain narrative of their case will not fail to excite pity and compassion.'

"The above Memorial is taken from authentic accounts sent from Uist and especially from the letters of Bishop Macdonald. As their case is very deplorable, whilst their constancy and resolution, especially in such poor country people, is most admirable, they are most earnestly recommended to the charitable assistance of all good Catholics into whose hands this relation may come, in his own name and in the name of all his colleagues, and of all the Missionaries of this kingdom by

"GEORGE DAULIS, *Coadjutor.*

"EDINBURGH, 27*th November,* 1771."

At the present date it may seem extraordinary that such proceedings could take place within the limits of the United Kingdom, but it must be remembered that the Clan system, in which the Chief was supreme, was still strong in the Western Highlands. He had the power of life and death over his clansmen, and for centuries that power had, in the main, been exercised with justice and moderation. Although the power of the Highland chief had been much restricted during the previous fifty years, still it was very considerable, and moreover there was no authority at hand to which appeal against it could be made.

To these same causes were due in great measure the hardships inflicted by enforced emigration, of which the whole of the Highlands was to be the scene for the next half-century. Had all the emigrations been conducted with the same forethought as those of Glenaladale from Uist, untold suffering would have been avoided, and many bitter memories on both sides of the Atlantic would have been saved. Moreover, the emigration itself would have succeeded far better, since nothing but tales of happiness and prosperity would have come back to those at home, instead of the sad tales of misery which only too often followed in the trail of enforced emigration.

Regarding the action of Boisdale it is a strange coincidence that his gross abuse of authority should have occurred at the very time when, in Edinburgh and

London, Government was granting large measures of toleration, and when the bishops in their letters to Rome speak of the favour they were enjoying from Government. Had such a misfortune fallen on these people one hundred years earlier, what would have become of the Catholics of Uist ?

Bishop Challoner had the Memorial printed at his own expense and distributed amongst the English Catholics. It had the desired effect, and everyone was much affected by the suffering and heroic constancy of the poor Highlanders. Public subscriptions were made for them in London, and a considerable sum was thus obtained. Bishop Macdonald and Bishop Hay united in thanking Bishop Challoner for his "amiable behaviour," and prayed God to reward him for his charity.

Bishop Hay also contributed largely out of his slender means, as well as by his pen. Glenaladale writes to him : " I do certainly admire the extent and heroism of your charity towards Boisdale's people ; could I persuade myself that you spared so much to them out of a superfluity rather than out of what seems your whole, I could easier reconcile myself to it."

In May, 1772, 210 emigrants sailed for St John's Island : 100 from Uist ; the rest from the mainland. They took with them enough meal for one year, and were accompanied by Mr James Macdonald, missionary priest. It was estimated that the cost of transporting the emigrants would be about £1,500, all of which they later most carefully repaid. They had a fine passage to America, where they arrived in seven weeks, with the loss of only one child. Mr James Macdonald sent Bishop Hay a most favourable account of the French colonists there, whom he represented as a set of excellent people and good Catholics. In 1776 Bishop Hay wrote to Bishop Geddes: " The Uist people are doing extremely well in St John's Island, coming fast on, and living already much better than at home."

After the departure of the emigrants, Clanranald interposed and insisted on obtaiinng from Boisdale religious toleration for the poor people who remained. The Pope also brought the matter to the notice of the young Duke of Gloucester, who was then living in Rome, and instructed the Nuncio at Paris to speak to the British Ambassador on the subject. The result was highly favourable to the Highland Catholics. The persecution was ended not only in Uist, but in other parts of the Highlands, where the proprietors had begun to follow the example of Boisdale.

Two years later, Mr Alexander Macdonald, priest of Barra, wrote to Bishop Hay: " 25th Sep. 1774. . . . Since our late terror and persecution, Boisdale is quite reformed, and is himself in all appearance the person who repents most for his former doings. He grants his people a most unlimited toleration in religious matters, welcomes our clergy always to his family, uses them with the utmost civility, and with the deference they are entitled to. His condescension is so great that we are allowed at times to perform some of our functions within the precincts of his ' palace,' for to be serious he has built such a genteel house, at Kilbride, South Uist, as I never expected to see in the Long Island."

The change in Boisdale's attitude towards the Catholic Church did not extend so far as to return to his religious duties ; or rather he seems to have deferred this until the last, and then the opportunity was denied him. His son, who had earlier been remarkable for his piety, and who was so zealous in the practice of his religion that he used to walk each Sunday the twenty miles to the old chapel at Gerinish, later became so bitter that he refused to allow the priest to enter the house when Boisdale was dying. Even the influence of Lady Macdonald, as Boisdale's wife was called, was unavailing. She was a daughter of M'Neil of Barra, and an excellent Catholic, of whom it is recorded that she used to say her prayers at the rock near Garrihellie, looking towards the chapel. On Sundays, Boisdale would walk half-way to church with her—she was his third wife—but she seems to have had no power against her stepson's determined refusal. Not only did he prevent his father from being reconciled on his death-bed, but he inscribed upon the tombstone that his father died a Protestant.

Like all the evicting and persecuting landlords, the Boisdales have long since disappeared from South Uist. Stranger still, when I was there in 1909, the " palace " of which Boisdale had been so proud was being taken down to build the cow-byres of recently settled crofters at Kilbride. The grandchildren and great-grandchildren of those evicted by Boisdale in 1770 were in many cases reinstated by the Crofters Commission on the farm of Kilbride about 1900. When the farm and policies had been apportioned among the crofters, the question arose what should be done with the house, which was still in very fair condition. The proprietrix (Lady Cathcart) stipulated that the house had to be pulled down, and it was bought by Mr Mackenzie, Lochboisdale, who sold most of the material later on. The " palace " of Boisdale was thus taken down and the materials sold to the crofters to be used in building their outhouses and cattle-sheds. *Sic transit gloria mundi !*

Another of the past glories of Uist is the ruin of Ormaclate Castle, the chief seat of Clanranald in the island. The present imposing ruin was built by Captain Allan Macdonald, who was killed at Sheriffmuir. It was here that Bishop Nicolson was entertained by the Catholic laird and his lady in 1700. To show the grandeur of the family of Clanranald at that time, it should be mentioned that they had another beautiful place at Borve Castle, Benbecula, close to the present chapel, and later a fine house at Nunton, three miles to the north. All these were, in addition to the grand old ruin of Castle Tirrim, in Moydart, always regarded as the real rallying place of the clan. As I pointed out on a previous occasion, all these lands have passed out of the hands of Clanranald and his relatives, with the single exception of Glenaladale, the property of the kindly helper of the evicted Uist crofters.

But to return to the succession of priests. Mr Alexander Macdonald was priest in Uist in 1779, and as such voted in the election of Bishop Alexander Macdonald. In 1782 Ranald Maceachan returned to Scotland from the Scots College, Rome. He was at once placed in Uist, where he continued till his death, which, to the great regret of his bishop, and indeed of all who knew him, happened in 1803. His death was caused by a complaint in the lungs, which arose from a severe cold he caught in the exercise of his missionary duties. He was a young man of great merit, and of more than ordinary learning. His excellent qualities made him to be loved and respected even by the Protestants. (Abbé Macpherson.)

Mr Maceachan was succeeded by Mr Roderick Macdonald. This venerable clergyman — says the Directory of 1870—was born in the island of South Uist in 1763. At seventeen he was sent to the Scots College, Valladolid, where he was ordained in his twenty-eighth year. On his return to Scotland, he was appointed to Badenoch, where he was priest for twelve years (1791-1803). He was then sent to the north end of South Uist, and Benbecula, where, after discharging the duties of a faithful and exemplary pastor, he died, on the 29th September 1828, in the family mansion of Garfluich, of which farm and lands his forefathers had been tenants or gentlemen tacksmen (a race of landowners now nearly extinct) for generations.

Mr James MacGregor was the next priest in the northern portion, and he remained in charge till his death—the long period of forty years. The following account in the Directory of 1850 reads as if it came from his pen, for he took a pardonable pride in the work he had accomplished in the parish. He worked at the chapel of Ardkenneth and at the dikes around it with his own hands, and by his own remarkable industry stimulated that of his people :—

ARDKENNETH, KILVANAN AND BENBECULA

The mission under Mr MacGregor's charge is naturally divided into three districts. Iochar (Netherland) in the centre, Kilvanan to the south, and Benbecula to the north.

Ardkenneth in Iochar. This chapel was erected in 1829. It is seated for 400 persons, but 800 may assist in it at

Mass without inconvenience. It has no gallery. The dwelling-house is merely a continuation of the walls and roof of the church, and the whole building measures 105 feet in length by 32½ feet in breadth over the walls. It is seen to a great distance in all directions, and has a very imposing appearance.

The inhabitants of this country speak their language (Gaelic) in great purity and with remarkable nicety. A place of worship, if it be large, and slated, they denominate Eaglais, a church. If the building be not large, but slated, they call it Caipball, a chapel; and a thatched place of worship they distinguish by the name of Tighe-pobuill, house of the people.

Kilvanan or *Cill-Bhainan*, dedicated to St Bain or Bainan, a thatched chapel, which stands about three miles south of Ardkenneth, was erected about the year 1820, by Mr Roderick Macdonald, a scion of the Clan-ranald family. It accommodates 300 persons.

Benbecula, to the north. Here is also a thatched chapel, which was built about 1790 by Mr Ranald Maceachan, cousin-german to the late Marshal Macdonald, Duke of Tarentum, and affords accommodation to about 400 persons. In its day it was thought a handsome building, but now the walls of it are failing, and something must be done to prevent it from becoming a complete ruin; but whence the means are to come it is difficult to say. Balie-Mhanich (Monktown), where the chapel stands, on the verge of the Atlantic, was in days gone by possessed by monks, of which fact some small traces are still to be seen.

Of the Clan-Donuil, that branch styled the Macdonalds of Castle Tirrim in Moydart, commonly called Clanranald, continued Catholics down to the year 1745, or for some years posterior to that period. To this circumstance, as a human cause, may be attributed the preservation of the Faith in their extensive territories—viz. Moydart, Arisaig, Isles of Eigg and Canna, Benbecula and South Uist. It is a fact that the Clanranald of the day occasionally procured priests from Ireland to supply the means of religion in this island. The last of these was Mr Wynn. . . .

The Clanranalds, since they abandoned the Faith, were not personally hostile to their Catholic tenants, but their factors, and the underlings of these factors, have done a vast amount of evil by artfully and covertly supplanting or ejecting the poor, helpless Catholics, and by introducing and fostering in their places Protestants from North Uist, Skye and Harris; while the Catholics have been expatriated and compelled to remove to more friendly climes. Since the year 1828 about 700 Catholics have emigrated from Mr MacGregor's mission to America, and still, notwithstanding this, the number under his charge is at present (A.D. 1850) not less than 2,000.

It will be best to continue the story of these northern chapels before returning to the southern end of the island. The chapel at Ardkenneth is much the same to-day as it was in the times of Mr MacGregor. The stone-cobbled floor is probably the only one now left in the Highlands, and when strewn with fresh sand has a neat, clean appearance, such as no other material procurable at that date would ever have had, after nearly a hundred years of continuous use.

Mr MacGregor died in 1868. He was born in 1790, entered Lismore Seminary in 1808, and was ordained in

1816.   He was priest at Fort William from 1819 to 1828, and was removed from there to South Uist.   In 1836 he went to Ireland to collect money for the erection of his church, which he had begun as early as 1829.   During his long residence amongst them, the people had become greatly attached to him, and deeply mourned his loss. In his later years he was assisted by Mr Colin Macpherson, and afterwards by Mr Donald M'Coll.

Mr Donald Mackintosh succeeded Mr MacGregor.   In 1872 he appealed for a new chapel in Benbecula. " Here," he says, " matters are very unsatisfactory. With a considerable congregation at a distance of six miles from Ardkenneth, the only chapel it could boast of was a very old structure, which had to be abandoned a few years ago.   The people have hitherto been attended by the priest from Ardkenneth, always with inconvenience, some-times with considerable danger to himself, owing to a perilous ford.   It is therefore proposed to form it into a separate mission and to build a chapel and priest's house."

The priest's house was finished in 1878, when the priest in charge appealed for funds to go on with the chapel. " An effort," he says, " will be made to replace the present miserable thatched chapel—the last but one of its kind in Scotland—by one more befitting its sacred purpose. The chapel is not only unsightly to a degree, but far too small, 300 people are often rather packed than accommodated in it."   As early as 1850 the Directory had stated : " In South Uist there are three slated chapels, erected through the exertions of Messrs MacGregor and Chisholm ; there is also one black chapel.   In Benbecula there is only a black chapel, a larger one is very necessary there."   (Note II.)

It is interesting to watch the growth of these chapels; what a couple of generations ago was the pride of priest and people, as in Moydart, Braelochaber and Kilvanan, is in these recent times looked upon—and certainly most justly—as little worthy of the services of the Church, and efforts are made to replace them by the very picturesque chapels which now adorn so many of the Catholic parishes in the West Highlands of Scotland. At the same time there has also, of course, taken place a vast improvement in the houses of the people and in their manner of life.

The new church in Benbecula was finished in 1884, and the account of the opening ceremony is very interesting. It was apparently a real Uist day, the rain falling in sheets, yet no less than sixteen miles of road and water had to be traversed by the greater part of the company. Little wonder that they had to encounter some difficulties. The following is the account in the Directory of 1885 :—

" About 100 miles N.W of Oban (the port for mails and for passengers to the Outer Isles) lies the Island of Benbecula, separated from the Islands of North and South Uist, by tidal fords of 3 and 1½ miles in breadth, respectively. These together with Barra, form what is locally known as the ' Long Island.' They have always contained a large Catholic population, who have carried down their Faith through all persecutions to the present time.

" In Benbecula alone there are over 700 Catholics. Two years ago the priest in charge found it necessary to ask for subscriptions for a new chapel, the old one of rude stone being in a ruinous condition. On 4th August last a large steam yacht, chartered by Mr Campbell, of Lochnell, left Lochnell Bay, with the Bishop and a numerous party ; they landed at Lochskipport, and from there drove to Benbecula, a distance of 14 miles. The following morning a large party of visitors came to Benbecula from South Uist amidst a downpour of rain. After some difficulties, necessitated by a longer route of 16 miles, the church was reached at 1 P.M. and Pontifical Mass was sung. Many priests and a large number of Islanders from all parts were present. The Islanders were rejoiced beyond description at seeing ceremonies which had been unknown in the island for centuries, and in their enthusiasm they followed his Lordship and the visitors for a long way on their return journey."

Since Benbecula was formed into a separate mission it has been served by Rev. Donald Mackintosh, now Provost of the Chapter ; by Rev. Alexander Macdougall (1891–1903), Rev. Hugh Cameron (1903–1908) and Rev. John M'Millan (1908–   ).   During the same period the parent mission of Ardkenneth was served by Rev. Donald M'Coll (1877–1887), Rev. Angus Macrae (1887–1903), Rev. Donald Walker (1903–1914), Rev. W. Gillies, 1915.

In the southern portion of the island Mr Ranald Macdonald was priest from about 1788 to 1819, when he was elected to succeed Bishop Æneas Chisholm as Vicar Apostolic of the Highland District.   During his stay in South Uist he built the old chapel and priest's house at Bornish ; the latter is still standing, and is situated about half-a-mile from the present chapel.   This was built by Mr John Chisholm, who, like Mr MacGregor, conferred untold benefits on the people of South Uist.   As my informant said : " Father Chisholm was Chief in Uist, where he had

CHAPELS AT—1. ARDKENNETH. 2. BORNISH. 3. DALIBURGH. 4. ERISKAY

To face page 48

great authority and the people dearly loved him; he was a pretty, pretty man, and a giant who could have thrown the factor—with whom he often had a disagreement—over the wall." At the time that the Bornish chapel was built there was a large congregation all around it, but the people were evicted in 1851. Since that date the chapel has stood alone, no house within a mile of it, and the larger part of the congregation, which still numbers about 500, four or five miles away. The scenes at these evictions were similar to those at Barra, Knoydart and elsewhere, and there is no need to repeat the harrowing details here. Suffice it to say that they have left memories of suffering and injustice which half a century has done little to efface. But happier days are dawning here also, for in 1913 the Board of Agriculture for Scotland came to an arrangement with the proprietrix, Lady Cathcart, whereby the three farms of Milton, Ormaclate and Bornish were made into small land holdings, and divided amongst the descendants of those evicted in 1851, who have never ceased to clamour for the land on which their forefathers had been settled for generations. One cannot but hope that a few years will see a thriving population in the district, clustering round their church, for which the people of Uist have always had such marked affection and veneration.

Amongst the benefits conferred by Mr Chisholm was the branch road down to Lochboisdale, which he was the first to propose. This was at the time of the famine. in 1846–1848. Mr Chisholm felt that the people were being supported by charity, and proposed making the road so as to give them employment, and the means of earning their food. At the meeting when this proposal was made,

D

the factor, Dr Alexander M'Leod, shook his fist in Mr
Chisholm's face, but he later sent an apology, when the
road had proved itself to be so great a boon. In reply
to the angry factor Mr Chisholm had merely whistled, a
favourite practice of his.

Mr Allan M'Lean was assistant to Mr Chisholm for a
short time, but went to America, where the following
incident occurred. He used to give of his fodder to a
poor neighbour, but the rogue was not content with what
he was given; he started to steal from the barn. The
servant, finding that fodder was going, complained to
Mr M'Lean, who decided that he should lock him in the
barn and he would watch for the thief. In due course the
rogue came in, made up his bundle, tied it over his
shoulder and made off. The priest went a short way
after him, for the stormy night prevented him from being
heard; he then lit the bundle from behind, and the storm
soon set it ablaze. The thief could with difficulty get rid
of the bundle, and not till he was badly burned. Next
day he went to the priest, who expressed surprise at seeing
him so badly burned. "Well, Father," said the thief,
"I thought I would do better for myself than what you
gave me; but the devil himself set fire to the bundle as
I stole it away last evening, and it's glad I am that I
saved my life from his clutches."

Mr Chisholm was very fond of the old customs, numbers
of which still survive, thanks in large measure to his
encouragement. A few are given here, such especially
as concerned the feasts of the Church. At Christmas
three Masses were said, one immediately after the other,
at midnight. Most of the men would bring their shinty
clubs even to the midnight Mass, and at dawn would go

—not home—but to the Machar for shinty. Even the old men would put off their shoes for the game, and there would be a small mountain of shoes at the goal. For the Christmas dinner, each household invariably killed a sheep, and had the best repast of the year.

On New Year's Eve boys and young men would go from house to house and would have to say their piece of poetry before the door would be opened. Then they would go round the fire by the left—the fire, be it noted, was always in the centre of the floor in those days—and before they sat down would say: " God bless the house and all its contents." To which Mr Chisholm or the oldest person present would say: " God bless you! God bless you!" This custom is still kept up.

For Purification, candles were made of tallow and ashes—peat ashes, needless to say—between folds of linen, and these candles were coloured blue, red, etc., to make them look festive. I brought back from Uist one of these candles and lit it at a meeting of the Society of Antiquaries at Inverness, when everyone was surprised to see how well it burned.

At Easter the children would go from house to house gathering eggs, and would then play amongst themselves. One would strike his egg against that of his opponent, and the winner would have whichever cracked People would rise early on Easter morning to see the sun rise, believing that it danced for joy.

St Michael's Day, or Michaelmas, was a great feast, and was kept as a holiday of obligation. Sports were held on the Machar, especially horse races, which took place at Ardmichel, a tongue of land midway between Bornish and Howbeg, and exactly half-way between the north and south ends of the island. In the evening there was a ball in every township. At Michaelmas also a special cake was made, one for each member of the family, and others would be sent as a remembrance to friends in Glasgow and elsewhere.

St Andrew's Day was the beginning of the shinty season, which afforded endless amusement during the winter afternoons, whilst the evenings were enlivened with song and story, the bagpipe and the fiddle, several of which may still be seen in almost every cottage. Little wonder that Catholic Uist should have been a happy home where the ancient ballads survived better than elsewhere.

By contrast we can learn to appreciate the efforts of our own clergy, whose conduct in this matter differed so greatly from that of many of their Presbyterian contemporaries. Mr Alexander Carmichael, who was far from being a Catholic, but who, as the greatest authority on matters Celtic in recent times, has every claim to our respect, bitterly regrets how the Calvinist ministers did their best by their stern disapproval to stamp out the old Gaelic poetry and customs. He gives instances of how the people of the Isles no longer dare to repeat the old tales to each other, though their minds are still so strongly tempered by them. One instance he quotes from a lady who, as a child, was sent to the parish school of Islay, to learn arithmetic from the schoolmaster. She used to join in the children's Gaelic songs and games, but as the schoolmaster, a narrow Presbyterian from the mainland, denounced Gaelic song and Gaelic speech, they could only enjoy them out of school time. " One day," she says, " the schoolmaster heard us and called us back. He punished us till the blood trickled from our fingers, although we were big girls with the dawn of womanhood upon us. The thought of that scene thrills me with indignation." Mr Carmichael himself was often tantalised by the story or song he had coaxed out of a Highlander being stopped midway by the appearance of the minister or one of the disapproving elders of the district. (*Dublin Review*, October, 1911, p. 338.)

The same spirit may be seen in the earlier Reports of the Society for Promoting Christian Knowledge, where frequently such passages as this occur : "If the people of this district are to be taught the true Gospel Teaching, they must learn English. The want of English is one of the chief causes why they remain in ignorance," where ignorance and Catholic teaching are often considered to be one and the same thing. Certain it is that the teachers sent from Edinburgh at the beginning of the last century were keenly opposed to Gaelic. There is the further fact that the Highland dress and Gaelic language were thought to be marks of the Jacobite, and Government wished to discourage everything that might lead to a recurrence of the " forty-five."

The same ideas occur in the Report of Messrs Hyndman and Dick, appointed by the General Assembly of the Church of Scotland to visit the Highlands and Islands, 1760. The Report is certainly very moderate in tone, while the concluding sentences are not a little striking. " In countries lying under such complicated disadvantages, it is easy to see the difficulty of extirpating ancient prejudices, and of introducing the Protestant Reformed Religion. The Roman Catholic persuasion, which was formerly established in this and every other part of Great Britain hath kept possession of many parts of the

Highlands ever since the Reformation. Notwithstanding
the discouragement given to it at different periods, the
zeal of the Church of Rome, together with the concurrence
of political causes, hath been hitherto able to preserve
and even on some occasions to strengthen that interest.
The priests of that Communion are numerous and active,
and although their salaries be small, yet the advantage
of a foreign education, which they receive from a publick
fund, and the influence which their political religion gives
over the minds of the people have contributed to check
the progress of the Reformation, and at some periods to
gain proselytes to their own Church."

On the death of Mr Chisholm, in 1867, his nephew,
Mr William Macdonell, returned to the Bornish mission,
where he had earlier spent several years as assistant
to his uncle. Mr Macdonell, who had previously built
the church at Knoydart, undertook a begging tour to
collect funds for rebuilding the church at Daliburgh,
seven miles south of Bornish. On his return he caught
a severe cold, died at Bornish, and is buried at Daliburgh.
The later priests of this mission were Rev. Alexander
Campbell (1871–1883), Rev. John Mackintosh (1883–
1900), Rev. Donald Morrison (1900–1903), Rev. William
M'Lellan (1903–1912), Rev. John Mackintosh (1912-   ).

Previous to 1868, when the present chapel was built
at Daliburgh, there was a slated chapel on the same site.
Previous to that again Mass used to be said in a crofter's
house still standing. A sign of the size of these chapels
is that when the present chapel was being built, the old
one was allowed to stand, the new walls were built round
it, and the roof placed over them, after which the old building was removed from within the new. The successive

priests who filled this mission were Rev. Donald M'Coll (1867–1874), Rev. Alexander Forbes (1875–1881), and, for shorter periods, Rev. Alexander Mackintosh, Rev. Allan McDonald, Rev. George Rigg, Rev. Samuel Macdonald, Rev. William Macdonald, Rev. Alexander Macdougall, who, in 1907, greatly enlarged the church and redecorated it.

The tale of self-sacrifice of Father George Rigg is very beautiful; he was in the thirty-sixth year of his age and the seventh of his priesthood. Day after day for several weeks he had been attending cases of fever and nursing the patients from morning till night, since no other person—not even the nearest relative—would venture within gunshot of the infected houses. One case was particularly noticeable—that of a poor old woman and her only son. They both sickened of the fever and had no one to attend them. Father Rigg was their only helper; he cooked their food, tidied the house, and mended the fire. The son died first, and he laid him in his coffin and attended him to the grave. After this he too caught the fever, and at the end of a week, despite the constant care of three doctors, he succumbed, having thus sacrificed his own life to save that of others, and to care for them in death. His own coffin was borne part of the way to the grave by the six neighbouring priests, and as the story of his heroic death became known great was the admiration which it excited, and loud the praise that was lavished on the young priest in the far-distant isle of Uist.

Father Allan McDonald, the apostle of Eriskay, as his people loved to call him, is another charming character to which it is difficult to do justice in the short space at my disposal. During the years he was at Daliburgh (1885–1894), he had come to know and to love the people of the little island of Eriskay, about 400 in number. There is indeed a great attraction about the island and its people. It has no road at all, all traffic, such as carrying peats, etc., being done by creels on the backs of ponies. Fishing is the chief means of livelihood, and this, in addition to the crofts, gives the people all they require. They are indeed remarkably happy and contented. There is no licensed house upon the island, and woe betide the fisherman who in Father Allan's time brought spirits to his beloved island home.

In 1887 Bishop Angus Macdonald, who had the greatest personal respect and affection for Father McDonald, issued the following appeal : "Rev. Allan McDonald, besides the Mission of Daliburgh, South Uist, numbering over 1,500 souls, has charge of an outlying district, the Island of Eriskay, separated from the main Island by a stormy channel and having a population of about 400 souls. His time and strength are more than fully taxed by the care of the principal mission ; whilst such occasional attendance as he is able to give to the Eriskay station, though quite inadequate to the wants of the poor people, involves a serious strain on his strength and danger to his health For the sake of both priest and people therefore the erection of Eriskay into a separate Mission is urgently called for. The present church, a wretched hovel, has been so far improved internally by his zeal, that it will suffice as a temporary arrangement until funds for a more suitable church are forthcoming. But a house for a resident priest is in the first instance needed, and I have authorised and indeed urged Rev. Allan McDonald, to endeavour to collect the necessary funds."

The house was built without much difficulty as to funds, and the church followed soon after, being opened in 1903. Then, just as he seemed to have secured all he could for his Eriskay flock, Father Allan was cut off by death, at the early age of forty-six. The story of his life and work are best told in the words of his obituary notice, though it cannot but be regretted that no biography has been written of one whose life was a constant source of edification and pride to his bishop, his fellow-priests, and to that wider circle of the literary world who, year by year, came to know and to respect him. His relations to his people also, whom he ruled no less sternly than he tended kindly, can find few parallels in the lives of the holiest priests. The obituary notice is given in full, as incidentally it affords much information on the conditions existing in the Western Islands :

" Rev. Allan McDonald was born in Lochaber in 1859 and was ordained in 1882. His first two years as priest were spent at Oban, and in July 1884 he was sent to Daliburgh in S. Uist. Here he had charge of a congregation of 2,200 souls, all with only two exceptions Gaelic-speaking, and natives of the island. Father Allan entered on his work with characteristic zeal and self-sacrifice in the midst of many difficulties and privations. The congregation was one of small crofters and fishermen—toilers of the land and sea—earning a living, precarious at best ; and unable, no matter how willing, to do much for the support of the priest. The conditions of life in the Hebrides at that time were little known and understood by dwellers on the mainland, and few knew

to sympathise with the priests in their peculiar local difficulties and in the hampering poverty of themselves and
of their people.   The present generation may know times
that are no worse than had been, they may meet with
more sympathy from without, and improved communication doubtless keeps them more in touch with the outer
world, but the fact remains that even now, for priest and
people, life in the Hebrides is made up of hardships and
trials which dwellers on the mainland little know or
understand.

"Father Allan's labours and zeal in attending to the
Catholics of Daliburgh was unceasing.   He also had the
charge of the 400 souls in Eriskay   Mass was said in
the island, in an old, thatched, dry-stone building by the
priest from Daliburgh.   Under the most favourable
circumstances this meant getting over five miles of road
and two of sea to reach Eriskay, 'wind and weather
permitting.'   It was often impossible to sail over to the
island and once there it was as often impossible to recross
and return home.   The regular visits and the frequent
sick calls entailed much hardship, and often a stay of
days and nights in Eriskay, waiting for weather in which
the boat could live.   There was then no house for the
priest in the island, and his people gave him willingly of
their best in food and shelter   Such was Father Allan's
life as a priest in Uist living for his people, and faithfully
doing his duty.   In temporal matters he was at their
service as a leader and adviser.   In an acute crisis regarding the land question, he guided his people wisely
and well, in their successful struggle to obtain fixity and
more reasonable conditions of tenure.

"But no ordinary constitution could hold out against

Father Allan's heroic labours, and after some years he
was forced to admit, that he was no longer physically
fit, for the duties of a Mission such as Daliburgh. He
had overtaxed his energy and his strength, and following
on a severe attack of influenza, weakness of the heart
made itself only too apparent. Through his exertions a
suitable Presbytery had been erected in Eriskay and the
island had been formed into a separate charge with
Rev. Donald Mackintosh as its first priest. Father Allan
was transferred to Eriskay in 1893. Here he was destined
to spend the remainder of his days, and here the record
of his life was the same; duty faithfully discharged, a
life spent for and with his devoted flock. He loved his
bare, tree-less, windswept island, he was with his people
in their joys and sorrows, his people loved and were
proud of their pastor. He was everything to his people
and they were everything to him.

" He had set his heart on building a suitable church
to replace the old thatched building that had done duty
for so many years. His people helped in the good work,
young and old, men and women, gave what they could
in the building of God's house. Those who owned boats
and nets promised one night's catch of fish toward the
cost of the new church and many and fervent were the
prayers that it might be a record one—and so it was.
The total catch realised a considerable sum, and one boat's
crew handed their pastor £50 as the proceeds of a single
night's fishing.

" In response to an appeal, aid came from without—
speedily and beyond all expectation. Sympathy was evoked
by the plain unvarnished statement of Eriskay's needs,
and this sympathy took practical form. Contributions

came in generously from rich and poor, priest and layman, and also from kind friends not of the household of the Faith. A commencement was made with the building and it was completed in a far shorter time than priest or people had dared to hope.

" But the completion of the church brought no rest to Father Allan. He became, if that could easily be, more anxious for their spiritual good, more attentive to his own priestly duties. He was moreover always in active sympathy with his people in all that concerned their temporal welfare. The houses were improved, bridle paths made—there are no roads nor ever have been—by the Congested Districts Board. Once a year he solemnly blessed the Eriskay fishing fleet and, by special permission of the Pope, said Mass on one of the boats to bring God's blessing on men and boats and fishing gear, ere starting on the season's work.

" Notwithstanding his busy life and impaired health, he was an indefatigable student of Gaelic and a recognised authority on all that related to traditions, whether Celtic or Norse, the folk-lore, fairy tales, antiquities and history, the fauna and flora, the shells and algae of the Hebrides. His publications were but few, yet he left MSS. amounting to thousands of pages, and it is hoped that some of these at least will be published and that Father Allan may some day be given the place among Celtic scholars which by every right is his. He gave—all too freely be it said—of his gleanings to other workers in the Celtic field. [I have heard it stated, but on what authority I do not recollect, that he was offered the chair of Celtic in the University of Edinburgh, if he would eave his island home, but nothing would induce him to leave his beloved Eriskay and its good and simple people]

" Remarkable it is that with all his culture, only once a year did Father Allan visit the mainland, which must have offered so many attractions to him. On these occasions after attending the meeting of the clergy he would return to Eriskay with as little delay as possible.

" His illness was of short duration, and his funeral was such as could be seen nowhere else. Immediately after the coffin walked the clergy, followed by the women and children, children on foot and children in arms, mothers and their families weeping and praying for the fond father who was making his last journey to his home in their midst ; the aged too, men and women all took part in that last act of veneration to one they loved so well." And when men were ready, as usual, to fill in the grave with spades, they were put aside by the Islanders, who sobbing, laid soil and sods gently with their hands over the coffin, and so the grave was filled and covered. Surely Father Allan would have thought himself well re-paid for living and dying amongst his devoted Islanders, to have received such a funeral, marked as it was by the most touching affection and the deepest veneration.

KNOYDART

THE first mention that we have of Knoydart, as far as Catholic life is concerned, is when Mr White, at the request of the Catholics there, blessed the waters of Loch Hourn, which divides Knoydart from Glenelg, and thereby brought back the herring to the loch which had formerly been noted for its fishing, but which, for some years previously, had yielded no return. The statement is interesting as proving, amongst other things, how great must have been the activity of Mr White, since almost every district bears witness to his zeal. This was about the year 1660.

In the Report of his Visitation in 1678, Mr Leslie says of Knoydart that the Catholics there were very numerous and very fervent. We find, indeed, that they formed one of the largest congregations of Highland Catholics until the evictions of 1852. In 1700 Bishop Nicolson passed from Glengarry into Knoydart,—probably following the route which for several years was a favourite one with the late King Edward,—along Loch Garry side, then through the beautiful hills which form the forests of Glengarry and Glen Quoich, ten miles along Loch Quoich, and thence to the head of Loch Hourn, where the road drops 500 feet to sea-level. At that time there was, of course, no road worthy of the name, and hence the Bishop's statement that although he had crossed and

62

recrossed the Alps, he had never experienced anything like the difficulties of this journey.

The Bishop spent one night at Loch Hournhead, and the next day he and his party went seven miles down the loch and were met by Lord Macdonell, " who conducted them with great civility to the house of one of his vassals,[1] where we had the ordinary prayers "—evidently an obscure manner of speaking of Mass. The Report goes on to say that "on the 9th August, the Feast of St Columba, Patron of the Highlands and Islands, we again had ordinary prayers, with Confirmation afterwards, and this we did wherever we went." Before leaving Knoydart they paid a visit to the old laird, who was nearly ninety-five years of age. He had greatly distinguished himself in the wars of Montrose, and being cousin to Lord Macdonell, had succeeded him in all his property. The fine old soldier received the Bishop with the greatest respect, and forced him to stay some days in his house, where about forty persons were confirmed, the rest being put off until the return of the Bishop from the Isles.

The same road was followed by Bishop Gordon in 1707, whose journey is thus described : " June 16th, the little party came to Glenquoich, and then their real difficulties began. They had to scramble sometimes on all fours, along rude mountain paths, beset with precipices and with morasses. Their feet were never dry. But the Bishop's cheerfulness kept up the spirits of the party. At the head of the Loch, they were met by Glengarry's brother, who conveyed them some miles in a boat to his

---

[1] This was Barrisdale, generally supposed to be the " Glennaquoich " of Sir Walter Scott's " Waverley."

house, there being no road practicable on shore. Here they remained a couple of days to rest; and on the 20th they arrived at the Laird of Knoydart's house, where the Bishop thought it at length safe to enter on the proper duties of his Visitation. The 22nd was a Sunday; the people were then called together, and Confirmation was administered to as many as were found prepared."

A month later, after visiting the Hebrides, Bishop Gordon returned, via Arisaig and Borrodale, to Knoydart, the road being a very rough and fatiguing one. At Scothouse, he ordained the young deacon, who had accompanied him from Preshome, as a missionary for the Highlands. It was the first ordination that had taken place in Scotland since the Reformation. On his way back to Glen Quoich, the Bishop began to feel the effects of his fatigues, and of insufficient food; he was detained two days on his journey by a slight attack of fever. On 1st August he reached Strathglass.

It was in 1907 that the present writer covered the same ground at the end of a walking tour. The previous days had been pleasant enough, the bright sun and the crisp air of the first week of May being very bracing. My companion was very keen on leaving the road and striking home across country; and as he had complied so far with all my suggestions I felt bound to consent to this, though I knew well that the track across the hills had a very bad name, and that if our host had been at home he would never have allowed us to attempt it. We left Glenelg Hotel—where the lessee, Mr Donald Mackintosh, had during many years placed his large house at the disposal of the neighbouring Catholics for Mass as often as the priest could come over—and started on our sixteen-mile tramp across the hills to Loch Hourn.

Following the course of the Glenbeg river, we passed Dun Troddan and Dun Telve, the Brochs or Pictish Towers, which are the delight of the antiquarian. As we began to mount the north side of Ben Sgriol (Screel) the thick mist which had been hovering round the top began to come down upon us, and in a few minutes we could not see a hundred yards in front of us. Fortunately I had a compass—a thing one should never be without when crossing hills in Scotland—and also an ordnance map, so we managed to strike the right spur of the hill and crossed at a height of about 2,000 feet. By this time we were wet to the skin, and the small flask and few biscuits, which were all we had brought, were finished. The map showed two shepherds' houses on the track, which at one time was much frequented by drovers taking their sheep and cattle to and from the Isle of Skye ; and at these cottages we intended to get the usual refreshment which all through the Highlands one finds so readily offered. Our hearts beat high as we neared the first one, the bright green of the grass around forming a striking contrast to the perpetual brown and iron colour of the peat moss we were crossing. We were already at the door before we noticed that this had long been off its hinges, the roof was just falling in, and all the windows were broken. It had evidently been un-inhabited for several years. My companion and myself prided ourselves on not being easily discouraged, but this —at a distance of ten miles from any other human habitation—fairly tried our pluck. It was useless to think that the other shepherd's house would prove more

E

fortunate—the hill had evidently been turned over from sheep to deer, and both houses would alike be tenantless— so we sat a few minutes in what had once been a warm; cosy kitchen, and then continued our cold, wet walk. It was five o'clock before we reached Kinlochhourn, and glad we were to get through the hills so soon. The head keeper would not believe that we had come across; he himself, he said, would never have attempted it. How- ever, he soon had a bright fire burning in the hearth, gave us dry shoes and stockings, a good warm meal, and insisted on our spending the night with him. Even when we had retired to bed my companion was so cold that I could hear the bed shaking as he shivered. He died of consumption a few years later, and I often wondered whether the first seeds of the disease were sown on that cold, wet tramp across the hills. It certainly was an instance of what the priests of old had, week after week, to undergo, as they passed from one holding to another amongst the hills.

It was only in the last century (1800–1850) that roads were made in the north-west Highlands, and even since they were made, the Highland priest has often to visit a shepherd's or a keeper's family far off the beaten track, when his experiences may, as likely as not, be just such as I have described. If Bishop Nicolson and Bishop Gordon found their visitations of the Highland district so trying, we may be sure that they were full of sympathy for the priests, whose lives, they knew very well, were largely composed of such incidents.

Regarding the priests who successively attended to the Knoydart district, we find Mr Munro stated to be priest of Knoydart in 1688. In 1689 Mr Cahassy is given as priest of Knoydart, Mr Munro probably confining himself to the Glengarry district, which adjoins it. In 1701 Mr Thomson's list gives Mr M'Lellan as priest of Knoydart, but he does not seem to appear in any later year. Mr Neil M'Phee was also there for some years, as also Mr Æneas M'Lachlan, who came to the mission in 1712. He is definitely stated, in 1728, to be stationed in Knoydart, and as we have all the districts accounted for in that year, he had probably been settled there for some time. He is again definitely stated to be there in 1733 and in 1736, and although the place of his residence is not given in the later lists in which his name appears, there is every reason to suppose that he remained in Knoydart till the troubles of 1745–1746. He did not leave the Highlands even during that period, and may, therefore, still have ministered to the people of Knoydart, for his name appears in the list of Highland clergy for 1755, though the place of his residence is not mentioned. He died in 1760, being then quite worn out by labour and the fatigues of the mission. In 1763 Mr Harrison had charge of Knoydart, and the two Morars, for Abbate Grant, the agent in Rome, writes: "The next district is that of Knoydart, which is a vast region of mountains, and being round in shape has about 12 miles diameter. Here there is not a single heretic, all the inhabitants being Catholic, to the number of 800 or 900. This district along with the two Morars have at present as Missioner, Mr William Harrison, an alumnus of the Scots College, Rome, who is now about sixty years of age."

In 1770 Bishop John Macdonald writes that he has just settled Mr Alexander MacDonald (*sic*) as priest in Knoydart, whilst his Report for 1777 states: "In the districts

of Knoydart and North Morar, Mr Alexander MacDonald
is priest.   He came from our Scots College, Rome, about
ten years ago, and is certainly young and strong ; but
considering the difficulties of his district, and its great
size, his work is too heavy.   It has indeed been increased,
by his own zeal and diligence, by two new districts, both
at great distances from his chief residence, the one at
Loch Arkaig to the East, the other to the North in the
country called Kintail.   Last year I administered Confirmation to about sixty of the people of this district,
all converted during the last four years.   I hope this
year to give him and another Alexander MacDonald, as
assistant, Mr James MacDonald, who came from our
College at Paris seven years ago, and is a strong active
young man."

. Although Bishop John MacDonald had been in Knoydart in 1776, he visited it again in 1779.   He then caught
an epidemic which was raging in the district, and after
only five days' illness he died, and was buried in Kilchoan
cemetery.   There are here two graveyards distant only
fifty yards from each other.   The one is nearly square,
and within this none but Catholics have ever been buried.
In the other, however, which is circular, there have been
burials of Catholics and Protestants alike.   It is in this
latter that the very interesting Celtic cross is standing,
whilst in the former there are three recumbent stones,
all with early Celtic designs.   After careful inquiry, I
was unable to ascertain in which cemetery Bishop John
was buried.   There is a vague tradition that the Celtic
cross marks his grave, but this is undoubtedly of much
greater antiquity.   A custom, however, is prevalent in
the district, of making fresh interments under these

venerable stones, and sometimes of moving them and placing them on recent graves. It is thus possible that the Celtic cross was used in this way to mark the grave of the good bishop. Another tradition makes the cross mark the resting-place of St Choan. Since the date of my visit, and in consequence of my representations, the proprietor had the ground which had accumulated round the foot of the cross cleared away. Unfortunately I did not know when the work was being done ; it would have been of great interest to discover the answer to these different points.

It was during the incumbency of Mr Alexander MacDonald that the first emigrations took place from Knoydart. In 1773 a large body of Highlanders emigrated from Glengarry and Knoydart at the invitation of the celebrated Sir William Johnston, to the then British province of New York, and settled in the bush of Sir William on the borders of the Mohawk river. At the outbreak of the revolutionary war the Americans tried every means to detain them in the country. When they found that entreaties, persuasions, threats and coaxing were of no avail they arrested several of the influential men and confined them in prison, but they contrived to effect their escape and, under the guidance of Sir John Johnston, son of Sir William, fought their way to the banks of the St Lawrence. During this expedition they suffered incredible hardships, both by hunger and fatigue, living chiefly on the flesh of their horses and dogs, and when that failed them, upon the roots of the forest. On their arrival in Canada they were formed into a corps under Sir John Johnston, and called the "Royalist Emigrants," and their services in the field contributed in a great degree to the preservation of Canada. At the conclusion of the war, as a reward for their services and in compensation for their losses, lands were granted them in Upper Canada, and they located themselves, some on the Niagara frontier, some on the Bay of Quinta, some on the shores of the St Lawrence, in what is now called the Johnston district, and others in the eastern district, in those counties now known by the names of Glengarry and Stormont.

Mr Alexander MacDonell, the priest of Knoydart, figured rather prominently in the election of a successor to Bishop John MacDonald The whole matter is placed before Propaganda by Bishop Hay, with his usual clearness and precision. He says: " I have always been of opinion that of all the Missionaries of the Vicariate he [Bishop Alexander MacDonald] was the most fit for that position. Moreover I have been confirmed in this opinion by the manner in which Mr Alexander MacDonell and his nephew have acted. This Mr MacDonell is certainly of one of the best families in the country, and related to many of our most influential Protestant gentlemen, and there is only too great reason to believe that in this matter he allowed himself to be persuaded that having been proposed by some of his brethren, he ought to be preferred before any one else to fill the place of the late Mr Tiberiop. [Bishop John MacDonald]

" Seeing that the affair was going contrary to his wishes he showed such displeasure as plainly proved that he was too attached to the vacant dignity. But his nephew, Mr Ranald MacDonell, of Scothouse, was not satisfied to show mere displeasure. Even after the decision of the Holy See he gave utterance to expressions so ignoble

that I would be ashamed to speak of them to your
Eminence, if he had not himself told me, that he had
sent also to your Eminence his unjust complaints in two
letters and had moreover written me several very insulting letters full of calumny, and accusing me of having
falsified the votes of the Missionaries to the injury of his
uncle. He also threatened me with the displeasure of
his non-Catholic relations. Other similar calumnies he
spread against the two deputies, not among the Catholics,
who well knew their falseness, but among the Protestants,
and even among official personages in order to obtain
through them an order from the Government to prevent
the execution of the Brief of his Holiness, in favour of
Monsignor Polemon (Bishop Alexander MacDonald).
It is an infinite sorrow to me, to have to relate such
things to your Eminence, and to see in our midst an
example so contrary to the spirit of our holy religion.
Still I have the satisfaction of assuring you that the
author of these troubles stands alone, that his proceedings are condemned even by Protestants, that our people
are very angry with him, and that the Missionaries of
that Vicariate have sent me a declaration, signed by
all except two, who have written to me separately,
since the common declaration could not be sent to them
by reason of their great distance. In this declaration
they all profess their full satisfaction and their perfect
submission to the choice of the Holy See in the selection
of Monsignor Polemon, and their entire disagreement
with the said proceedings to the contrary. Thus the
affair being now ended, I hope that these two will return
to their duty peacefully." It is pleasing to note that
Mr Alexander MacDonell later made a complete apology

to Bishop Hay, whilst Bishop Alexander MacDonald during his episcopate of twelve years proved himself to be only too self-sacrificing and disinterested.   He wore himself out in his labours to assist his clergy and their people, and died, universally regretted, at the early age of fifty-five.

Mention was made in a letter of Bishop John MacDonald of the recent converts in Kintail.   On 30th May 1777 he writes again from Duchanis: " I had the pleasure of receiving yours a few days ago, on my return from Kintail, where I was administering the Holy Chrism to our new converts there.   I think they are about sixty beside children, and are an entirely new acquisition except one family.   This place is visited from time to time by Mr Alexander, in Knoydart, who is nearest to them.   There is moreover great prospect of increase if they could be attended to, as is the case mostly in all countries bordering upon us.   There is considerable alarm taken at this newly sprung Congregation."

Further incidents in the Catholic history of Kintail are given in another letter of Bishop John, dated 7th April 1778, where he says that Archibald M'Rae of Ardintoul had written to him stating that serious perse-cution was to be feared on account of his sister's marriage with Conchra, and that Seaforth was much annoyed at the incident.   Also there was much ado about the " mighty affair of the tents."   " The affair of the tents " was this: " A great number of vessels and boats from all quarters convened to an arm of the sea in Kintail to fish herrings, amongst whom was a considerable number from our country.   Those who have only open boats make tents of their oars and sails on the shore to shelter them.   It happened that when Mr Alexander MacDonell

was at Ardintoul, the shoal of herrings moved to the part
of the bay which is contiguous to that place. The fishers
followed it thither, and all who used tents pitched them
there, the ground being very suitable for that purpose,
all along the beach. The next day being Sunday the
Catholics convened to Divine Service, which was performed in a private house, and the Protestants flocked
also thither from curiosity as they commonly do."
Unfortunately the letter does not tell us what was the
end of the matter, but at least it gives us a pretty picture
of the Catholics of those days. I shall have more to say
of the Kintail district later.

Bishop Alexander MacDonald, in his Report for
1783, states: " The next mission North of Morar is
that of Knoydart, 24 miles long and 6 broad, but on
account of the mountainous nature of the ground it is
not thickly populated. Still all the people in it are
Catholics, to the number of 1,042, not counting about
forty others in the districts round about. This Mission
would really require two priests if we had them, but
with our short numbers, Mr Alexander MacDonald has
the sole charge." Three years later (1786) he writes
again : " After Easter I visited the district of Knoydart,
for the 500 Catholics, who, as we said before, had gone
to America, were then about to sail. We cannot indeed
stop these emigrations, but we foresee that they will
injure our Missions a great deal, and have already done
so. For those who emigrate, are just the people who are
a little better off, and from whom the priest received
hospitality whilst on his journeys. Those who remain, on
the other hand, are mostly those who could not afford
the cost of emigration, and are also quite unable to help

the priest. Hence it happens that the condition of the priests grows daily more difficult, and this is naturally a great anxiety to me."

Mr Alexander MacDonald was succeeded by Mr Austin Macdonald. This latter writes, in 1787, that in consequence of the emigration of the people of Knoydart, " along with their priest," it fell to him to attend to those who remained. "Altho' there went to America not less than 600 Catholics, I administered the Sacraments to some 500 persons who remained." In the following year he writes again : " For seventeen years I laboured in the district of Moydart, but for the past two years, with the consent of my superiors, I have removed to that of Knoydart. Here formerly Mr Alexander MacDonald was stationed, a pupil of the Scots College, Rome, but he has gone to America with 604 of his parishioners. I find that there are still in this district about 500 communicants, not counting children. They are Catholics of good and simple lives and most steadfast in the Faith. Six miles distant from them is the district of Kintail, where only twenty years ago, there was but one Catholic family. At present there are from 300 to 400 converts also steadfast in the Faith, although they are as yet but imperfectly instructed. It has fallen to me to take charge of this Mission also, and I am only too pleased to do so, since there cannot as yet be a resident priest."

Mr Austin Macdonald was still priest in Knoydart in 1794, but about the year 1800 he went with some Highland emigrants to America, and died there soon after. He was succeeded by Mr Charles MacDonald, whose incumbency in this mission extended over a period of nearly forty years—that is, from 1797 to 1835. At the

time he was appointed—so runs the account of 1850—
there was not a more numerous nor a more respectable
congregation in the Highlands than that of Knoydart.
But its members, in consequence of successive emigrations, have now dwindled away to between 600 and 700
souls. Mr Charles MacDonald was succeeded in 1835
by Mr Neil MacDonald, who remained till 1847, when he
was succeeded by Mr William MacDonald. Mr Colin
Macpherson was appointed in 1850, and Mr Coll Macdonald
in 1851. It was during his incumbency that the greatest
troubles fell upon the Catholics of Knoydart, and Father
Coll was well qualified to face the distressing circumstances. The following is taken from his obituary notice
in the Directory for 1891. " Rev. Coll Macdonald was
born in Lochaber in 1812, and was known throughout
the Highlands as 'Father Coll.'" He entered Propaganda
in 1845 and was ordained in 1850 in Rome. He returned
to Scotland and was first stationed in Canna, where he
gave ample proofs of his missionary zeal. To quote
only one instance, may be mentioned the fact of his
crossing over on a Sunday morning from his island mission
to the mainland (a distance of nearly forty miles) in an
open boat—fasting, of course—and in weather more
than threatening, in order to give the poor people of
Knoydart an opportunity of attending Mass.

" In June, 1851, he was transferred to Knoydart, where
he spent the next four years of his ministry. They were
years of trial and sorrow to both pastor and people, for
it was shortly after his arrival at his new sphere of labour
that the then Proprietrix of the immense Glengarry
estates (of which Knoydart formed a part) commenced
the series of wholesale evictions which caused such

widespread suffering and distress throughout the country. Nearly 1000 members of Father Coll's poor and scattered flock were forcibly ejected from their holdings, their dwelling houses being torn down and burnt, and the barns and byres in which they took refuge being pulled down about their ears. During these scenes of violence, Father Coll never ceased to exert himself by every means in his power on behalf of his unfortunate people ; and when protest proved unavailing, he took active steps to organise a relief fund in their aid. Many of the emigrants he provided with food and clothing at his own expense ; and for those who remained, now destitute and homeless, he procured tents as a temporary shelter, some seven or eight families being thus lodged for some time in his own small garden. In 1854 when the work of eviction was over, the number of Catholics in the district was reduced to little more than seventy. A resident priest was thus thought to be no longer necessary, and Father Coll was accordingly transferred in the following year to Fort William. His name however was not forgotten amongst those whom he had befriended ; and for many years the newly arrived settlers in Canada, were accustomed to baptize their sons by the familiar name of Coll, in memory of the kind pastor whom they had left behind them in the Highlands of Scotland."

It may be thought that the above is an exaggerated picture of the Knoydart evictions, but if those interested in the subject will turn to the pages of Mackenzie's " Highland Clearances " they will find full details of really shocking cruelty. One or two instances must suffice here.

" Donald Maceachan, a cottar at Aror, married, with a wife and five children. This poor man, his wife and

children, were fully twenty-three nights without any
shelter but the broad and blue heavens. They kindled
a fire and prepared their food beside a rock, and then
slept in the open air. Just imagine the condition of this
poor mother, Donald's wife, nursing a delicate child,
and subjected to merciless storms of wind and rain during
a long October night. One of the melancholy nights
the blankets that covered them were frozen and white
with frost.

"Alexander Macdonald, aged 40 years, with a wife
and family of four children, had his house pulled down.
His wife was pregnant; still the levellers thrust her
out, and then put the children out after her The husband
argued, remonstrated and protested, but it was all in
vain; for in a few minutes all he had for his (to him
comfortable) home was a lot of rubbish, blackened
rafters and heaps of stones. The levellers laughed at
him and at his protests, and when their work was over
moved away, leaving him to find refuge the best way
he could. Alexander had, like the rest of his evicted
brethren, to burrow among the rocks and caves until he
put up a temporary shelter amid the wreck of his old
habitation; but from this also he was repeatedly driven
away. For three days Alexander Macdonald's wife lay
sick beside a bush, where, owing to terror and exposure
to cold, she had a miscarriage. She was then removed
to the shelter of the walls of her former house, and for
three days she lay so ill that her life was despaired of.
These are facts as to which I challenge contradiction. I
have not inserted them without the most satisfactory
evidence of their accuracy.

"John Mackinnon, a cottar, aged 44, with a wife and

six children, had his house pulled down and had no place
to put his head; consequently he and his family, for
the first night or two, had to burrow among the rocks
near the shore! When he thought that the factor and
his party had left the district, he emerged from the rocks,
surveyed the ruins of his former dwelling, saw his furniture
and other effects exposed to the elements, and now
scarcely worth the lifting. The demolition was so complete that he considered it utterly impossible to make
any use of the ruins of the old house. The ruins of an
old chapel, however, were near at hand, and parts of the
walls were still standing; thither Mackinnon proceeded
with his family, and having swept away some rubbish
and removed some grass and nettles, they placed a few
cabers up to one of the walls, spread some sails and
blankets across, brought in some meadow hay, and laid
it in a corner for a bed, stuck a piece of iron into the wall
in another corner, on which they placed a crook, then
kindled a fire, washed some potatoes, put a pot on
the fire and boiled them; and when these and a few fish
roasted on the embers were ready, Mackinnon and his
family had ONE good diet, being the first regular meal
they tasted since the destruction of their house!
Mackinnon's wife was pregnant when she was turned
out of her house among the rocks. In about four days
she had a premature birth; this and her exposure to
the elements, together with the want of proper shelter
and nutritious diet, has brought on consumption from
which there is no chance whatever of her recovery.

" One would think that as Mackinnon took refuge amid
the ruins of this most singular place, he would be left
alone, and that he would not any longer be molested

by man. But, alas, that was not to be! The manager
of Knoydart and his minions arrived, and invaded this
helpless family, even within the walls of the sanctuary.
They pulled down the sticks and sails he had set up within
its ruins—put his wife and children out on the cold
shore—threw his tables, stools, chairs, etc. over the walls
—burnt up the hay on which they slept—put out the fire
—and then left the district. Four times have these
officers broken in upon poor Mackinnon in this way,
destroyed his place of shelter, and sent him and his
family adrift on the cold coast of Knoydart. When I
looked in upon these creatures last week I found them
in utter consternation, having just learned that the
officers would appear next day, and would again destroy
the huts. The children looked at me as if I had been
a wolf; they creeped behind their father, and stared
wildly, dreading I was a law officer. The sight was
most painful. The very idea that in Christian Scotland,
and in the nineteenth century, these tender infants should
be subjected to such gross treatment reflects strongly
upon our humanity and civilisation. Had they been
suffering from the ravages of famine, or pestilence, or war,
I could understand it and account for it, but suffering
to gratify the ambition of some unfeeling speculator
in brute beasts, I think it most unwarranted, and
deserving the condemnation of every Christian man.
Had Mackinnon been in arrears of rent, which he was
not, even this would not justify the harsh, cruel and in-
human conduct pursued towards himself and his family.
No language of mine can describe the condition of this
poor family; exaggeration is impossible."

The writer then goes on to give numerous similar

instances, and justly remarks that additional hardship is added by the remembrance that all these poor evicted people were the descendants of those who for many genera- tions had been the faithful adherents of their persecutor, fighting his battles and defending his person, and in return looking to him as their protector and their father. When we think of the affection which for centuries the clansmen had shown for their chiefs, it is most sad to find the un- feeling return which was made to them. Mr Mackenzie also gives instances of the sufferings of those who, how- ever unwillingly, obeyed the orders to emigrate. There was the journey of three or four weeks in a crowded emigrant ship, remembered with horror by those who have ever undergone it, the landing in a strange country, where employment was often difficult to secure, and years of poverty and servility for those who had been accustomed to their own little plot of land and their quiet, independent life. But of these we shall treat more fully elsewhere. It should be noted, moreover, that this treatment had in most cases nothing sectarian about it. Evictions were carried out in almost every district of the Highlands, though it sometimes happened that the Catholic crofters, differing from the laird in religion, were harder dealt with than their Protestant neighbours. The foregoing instances are given by a Protestant writer, when dealing with the Highland clearances in general; but whereas the whole population of Knoydart was at that time Catholic, the persons evicted were almost certainly of that Faith. It is also impossible to avoid the subject —unpleasant though it be—as it alone was responsible for the almost entire removal of the Catholic congregation in this and other districts. We should remember, too, that only twenty-five years later the injustice of these removals was acknowledged by the passing of the Crofters Act, which grants fixity of tenure to the crofter so long as he pays his rent and complies with other moderate conditions. What would the Catholic population of Knoydart be to-day if the Crofters Act—now universally acknowledged to be a most just measure—had only existed to save its people.

The Directory of 1855 has this sad announcement: " As the Catholics of this Mission have, with the exception of a mere handful, been evicted from their holdings and left to perish on the hill-side, or driven to seek in some foreign land, a shelter which was denied them in the land of their fathers, the Bishop has been compelled to withdraw the priest, and to attach what still remains of a venerable and flourishing Mission to North Morar. It is only five years since several hundred pounds were expended in building a commodious chapel and house in this district, neither of which is now of any use."

Regarding the church buildings, previous to 1849 the services had been conducted in a long thatched house at Samadlan, where the priest's house is still standing, though the chapel has been almost entirely removed for building dykes, etc. Until recently, however, the walls were fairly high, and as one party expressed it, " the bracken was growing through the doorway, just as if people were coming out of church." There had also been a chapel at Inverie itself, " for at that time Knoydart was full of people from one side to the other."

In 1849 Mr William Macdonald built the church and house at Sandaig, which was then in the centre of a populous district. Its situation in the Bay of Sandaig

F

facing due south, and beautifully sheltered by the high ground on three sides of it, is most picturesque. At the time of my visit it was tenanted by two old maids, who had managed to stay on there in spite of all threats to turn them out. A charming picture was presented by these two old ladies, born as they had been alongside the chapel at Samadlan, and now living in their old age in the deserted chapel-house at Sandaig. Daily the elder of the two would walk two miles each way to their little croft at Aror. Here they kept a couple of goats, the milk of which, though barely half-a-pint, was the greatest dainty in their simple fare. Though there was but one house within two miles of them, the dear old people still clung to the ground they knew so well, and nothing would induce them to move to the village, four miles distant.

Knoydart had been attached to Morar for some years, when in 1884 it was again given a priest of its own in the person of Rev. John MacElmail, who was sent, as he states, " to keep alive the Faith among the 200 Catholics who still remained scattered over a wide area." In the Directory for 1887, after mentioning that Knoydart had at one time contained a large Catholic population, but that it had for some time been attached to Morar, the notice continues : " The priest on whom they now depended was separated from them by a stormy and dangerous arm of the sea ; his energies were fully taxed by the care of his own Congregation, and he could only rarely and with difficulty visit them, scattered as they were, over an exceptionally wide district of country. Yet they clung to their religion with devoted fidelity. Latterly, in response to their repeated solicitations, and finding that their numbers

FORMER CHAPEL AT SANDAIG, KNOYDART

To face page 82

had grown to nearly 200 souls, the Bishop formed the district into a separate Mission, although there was no prospect of its being self-supporting. Sandaig, the once populous locality in which the church and chapel house stood, had been changed by the cruel evictions into a silent wilderness, and the new pastor quickly realised the necessity of having a church in a more suitable position. But means were absolutely wanting wherewith to carry out the work, until Providence vouchsafed the opportunity through the generosity of Mr Louis de Gonzague Bailairge, Q.C. Quebec, who gave a donation for the erection of a church in honour of St Agatha. An excellent site was acquired at Inverie from Mr John Baird, the then Proprietor of Knoydart, who has all along evinced a friendly interest in the Catholics who form the bulk of his tenantry. The building which was commenced in 1885 was opened in September last. It stands on an eminence looking out on the broad waters of Loch Nevis, amidst scenery of the grandest description." Thus the district of Knoydart seemed to take a fresh lease of life, and the small remnant of her former Catholic population had all that their forefathers valued so highly, their resident priest and their pretty little church, to which they and all the Catholic Highlands have ever shown such great veneration and affection. The priests in later years have been Rev. George Rigg, Rev. William Macdonald, Rev. Arch. MacDonell, Rev. Wilfred Gettins

The daughter mission of Kintail continued to prosper. In 1822 Bishop Ranald MacDonald states : " In Kintail where we started a Mission not very long since there are at least 200 Catholics, besides those who have emigrated. They are under the charge of Mr Christopher MacRae,

a native of the place, now an old man, and a former
student of Valladolid." In 1831 Mr MacRae was still
priest here, and he continued in the mission till his death,
in 1842, at the age of seventy-eight. A couple of years
later Mr James Lamont was appointed to the mission,
which was then a very poor one, but Providence smiled
graciously on this district also, and sent a generous
benefactor in the person of the Duchess of Leeds, who,
at her sole expense, built a new church and priest's house,
along with a large building, where for many years the
Sisters of Mercy had a boarding-school, until the district
was found to be too remote for that purpose. The church
at the time of its opening in 1860 was the prettiest
church in the Highlands, and there is little wonder that
good Father Lamont was proud of it. In the account of
the opening ceremony he could not refrain from thinking
of the past, " when during seventeen years he had often
to travel as much as 40 miles on foot to a sick call
through piercing wind and snow. His chapel has hitherto
been a thatched barn like a hovel, neither wind nor
water tight, and his dwelling house scarcely better."
But these times have passed away, and although the
climate is no doubt severe in winter, still many a priest
from other parts has spent a pleasant holiday with the
priests of Kintail in their fine well-built house, with its
very pretty church alongside. The present writer must
confess to a great liking for Kintail, where he spent many
most enjoyable days, and that as late in the year as
October and November. One could always have a sail
on the loch, which comes up almost to the door of the
house, or a couple of hours' excellent sport, fishing in the
sea of an evening, or a walk along the sides of Loch

Long to the beautiful Falls of Glomach. If one took the Loch Duich road, one was always welcomed by the kindly hostess at Glen Shiel, an excellent example of the old type of Highland lady, who made you feel that you were doing her an honour in coming to call. No Highland priest will grudge a word of gratitude to good Miss Mackintosh, who, along with her brother, Donald Mackintosh of Glenelg, did so much to cheer the weary winter months of successive priests of Kintail, and in summer sought to welcome to their large and hospitable houses any priests from other districts whose short holiday brought them that way. Every priest who called was welcome to stay as long as he liked; he was cared for with that affectionate reverence which gave such virtue to the deed, and when he left no other payment would on any account be accepted, but the promise of a prayer and a blessing. It is a pleasure to be able to make this small return and this heartfelt acknowledgment for so much kindness on behalf of myself and of many, many other priests in the Highlands.

The later priests in Kintail were Mr Macdonald, the late Canon Bisset, Rev. Archibald Chisholm, Rev. J. Angler, Rev. George Grant, Rev. J. M'Lellan. Of these, Canon Bisset was here for over twenty years, and he ever looked back on his Dornie days as the happiest of his long priestly career. He was well acquainted with the traditions of the past two or three generations, and these pages were to have been submitted to him for revision, if death had not taken him away before they were finished. He died on 13th June 1915 in the seventy-sixth year of his age, and the fifty-third of his priesthood.

MORAR

THE district of Morar was, already in 1700, the recognised meeting-place for the few Catholic priests who then attended to the Catholics of the Highlands of Scotland. Bishop Nicolson, in the Report of his visitation made in that year, says : " On the 13th June we arrived at Eilean Ban, on Loch Morar. This is a fresh-water loch, having the district of Morar-mhic-Alisdair on the north and that of Morar-mhic-Dughaill on the south. Here, after consulting with Mr Cahassy, whose infirm state of health obliged him to stay on this island, and with Mr Rattray and some other priests, the Bishop sent all of them back to their own districts except Mr Morgan and Mr Maclellan, whom he decided to take with him to the Isles to serve as interpreter and to help in the functions." The party then sailed for the Outer Hebrides, and after six weeks returned to the mainland. The Report continues : " After our return from the Isles (on 29th July) we began the Visitation of Arisaig, Moydart and Morar and in the eight stations in this neighbourhood 700 persons were confirmed. Next day we drew up rules for the Catholic school that is in Arisaig, and then we went to Eilean Ban, in Morar, where we met the neighbouring Missioners and after consultation with them we drew up some disciplinary measures and regulations."

The foregoing paragraph enables us to correct the list of clergy in the Appendix to Gordon's " History of the

Catholic Church in Scotland." Under 1701 we find Mr Cahassy entered as "Moray," evidently intended for Morar, as the whole context above shows. Mr Macklen (*sic*), who is given as being in Knoydart, we find to be Mr Maclellan, as above ; Mr Munro (*alias* Rattray) and Mr Morgan are given in the list correctly, but the name Hackeen (*sic*) should be M'Eachen and Laggan should be Logan, this name being correctly given in the list for the previous year.

At the time of the Visitation of Bishop Nicolson, Mr Cahassy had been twenty-one years on the Highland mission, having come in 1681, and he seems to have been all this time in the neighbourhood of Morar, for in 1689 he is described as priest of Knoydart. He died in 1704, when his short obituary notice states : "He died in September. He was an Irishman, and did a great deal of good in the Highlands." He was succeeded by Mr Peter Fraser, who had been ordained in Scotland in 1704. In 1728 he was priest in Morar, assisted by Mr Dalgleish. Some further details are given by Bishop Geddes. "Mr Peter Fraser had been a dragoon and a Protestant ; he was wounded somewhere abroad and during the time of his cure met with great humanity from Catholics. This made him examine their religion, which he embraced. I think I have heard that he studied some time in Paris. He was ordained Subdeacon by Bishop Nicolson, 2nd December, 1703 ; deacon, 31st January, 1704, and Priest, 11th March, 1704. He was at Fochabers in 1715 ; in Glenlivet 1718 ; in the Highlands 1720, and particularly in Morar in 1728. He died in March, 1731." I would suggest that it was due to the troubles consequent on the Rising of 1715 that he removed to the Fochabers district, or he may only have been there to meet the Prefect of the mission, who often resided at Fochabers at this period, under the protection of the Dukes of Gordon, whose residence at Gordon Castle is close to Fochabers.

We have more details of his companion, Mr George Douglas or Dalgleish. According to Abbé Macpherson, "he came from the Diocese of Ross, and went to the Scots College, Rome, in 1698, aged 17; but at Bishop Gordon's desire he left it, being only a deacon, in 1706. The Bishop placed him for some time in a community at Paris, called Notre Dame des Virtus, to learn the practical duties of a missioner. In the latter end of the same year he went to Scotland and knowing well the Gaelic language, accompanied Bishop Gordon on his first visit to the Highlands, and was by him ordained priest at the House of Scothouse, on 25th July, 1707. He was an able missioner and did much good in the Highlands, where he laboured with great success for 24 years. He died in April, 1731." To these details Bishop Geddes's account adds the following :—" He was in the Highlands in 1715, and particularly in Morar with Mr Peter Fraser in 1728. For some years before his death (1731) he had not been able to say Mass on account of the palsy; but he heard confessions, gave instructions, and was also employed in going journeys on offices relating to the Mission, carrying money and the like." There seems something pathetic in the two invalid priests dying within a month of each other, but beyond the date of their deaths, no further details have come down to us.

Some years previous to this, Bishop Gordon had fixed on Morar for the site of his seminary. The first mention of a seminary is in 1712, in the correspondence between the Bishop on the one hand and Lewis Innes and Thomas Innes on the other. In 1712 Mr George Innes came home priest from Paris; he arrived in Edinburgh in bad health, and spent some time in his father's house, suffering from asthma and ague. Bishop Gordon designed him for the first Superior, and when he went on his tour through the Highlands in the summer of 1714 he had the pleasure of setting on foot his little Scalan in Loch Morar, though it was late in the autumn when Mr Innes was able to take charge of it. There were seven students in it, of whom Bishop McDonald, son of the laird of Morar, was one. This was West Scalan—a name often used afterwards for Samalaman. The Rising of 1715 put an end to it, and no attempt was made for some time to revive it.

Indeed, Bishop Gordon shortly afterwards opened the seminary in Glenlivet, and having fully as much affection for the Highland portion of his vicariate as for the Lowland—and this all his letters amply prove—he would have sent the Highland youths to the Glenlivet seminary. But when the Highland district was separated from the Lowland, and given a bishop of its own in the person of Bishop Hugh McDonald, this latter at once recognised the fitness of having a school or seminary of his own. Another reason which led him to this conclusion was the number of Catholic youths who were attracted to the schools recently founded by the Society for the Propagation of Christian Knowledge. " At this period," remarks Mr Thomson, in his Notes, " the greater part of the Missionaries in the Highland Vicariate were Scots or Irish religious who were bound by no ties to the Mission, and might at any time tire of its laborious life—as indeed only too many did." Bishop McDonald again fixed on the island in Loch Morar for the site of the school, chiefly because it was in an entirely Catholic neighbourhood. In June, 1732, he had several boarders, who did not intend to embrace the ecclesiastical state, and also four youths training up for the colleges abroad.

It will be interesting to note that the cost of each pupil at this time was £6 a year at Scalan, according to the statement of the bishops in the letter to Cardinal Spinelli, Prefect of Propaganda. The whole question as to the need of a seminary is fully discussed in the first letter of the new Highland bishop to the Cardinal Prefect of Propaganda. It is dated 18th March, 1732. He says : " Relying on this kindness on the part of your Eminence to me, as soon as I was consecrated—which event took place in Edinburgh—I hastened to the Highlands, and especially to those parts which seemed most to require the care and solicitude of the Bishop. These districts, to say the least, did not allow me to be idle, so great was the distress of the faithful in consequence of the dearth of Missionaries. When I had worked there for a few months the sad state of affairs revealed itself. Wide tracts of country which have of necessity been assigned to single priests on account of the scarcity of these, far exceed the capacity of the most diligent pastors. Necessity obliged that in the place of some who had died, other Missionaries should be brought from the south, but these, even though they were of Highland origin, were ignorant of the language, having forgotten it while they studied abroad ; they were thus almost useless. The faithful greatly bewail the scarcity of priests and grieve that while those in other parts enjoy all spiritual comforts, they themselves suffer the greatest need, not from any want of diligence on the part of the labourers, but from the scarcity of these. . . . Whilst I ponder over a remedy for so great an evil, this seems to me the most efficacious—that a seminary be started in this Highland District for the training of youths suitable for the ecclesiastical state. It will thus happen that the youths who will in future be sent to the colleges abroad will be better prepared, whilst others, being ordained in this country, will make up for the small number of those who come back as priests from the colleges. How comes it indeed that of the Highland youths who, after the most careful selection, have been sent abroad, so large a proportion give up the ecclesiastical state, and, returning to the vanities of the world, belie the hopes which had been placed in them?

" If however only those are sent abroad who have been tried in the seminary and who have made some progress in study at college, it is to be hoped that more will complete their studies and attain to the priesthood. If to these be added such as will be entirely educated in this country, it is to be hoped that there will at length be a supply of priests sufficient to satisfy the demands of both Catholics and well-disposed heretics. On the other hand it is plain to me that without such an institution our holy faith will never make much progress, whilst there is great danger that from the dearth of priests—of which we shall always have to suffer, unless the seminary be started—many of the weaker among the faithful be led away by the arts and devices of the crowd of heretical ministers, catechists and schoolmasters who are daily being forced upon the people.

" Our Catholic Highlanders however, are so poor that there is no hope of our beginning this most useful and most pious work unless your Eminence lend a helping hand. I cannot but commend the whole matter to the zeal and charity of your Eminence, for if it fail, not only will all our labours be in danger of proving fruitless, but we clearly foresee the loss of countless souls. I am on the point of visiting the Hebrides and other distant places, and shall omit nothing which may help towards starting the seminary as soon as possible, trusting to the generosity of your Eminence, which has already been so great towards me, and which I hope will never fail our pious labours and endeavours."

In the following year Bishop McDonald again begs the help of Propaganda for his seminary in the west. He also thanks the agent, Mr William Stuart, for his promise of 300 livres a year in support of it. Evidently the good agent had been touched by the Bishop's moving appeal. The letter continues : " I hope since Exchange promised to give something for that purpose, you'll insist more and more for obtaining it, for I have begun the good work, having made up a large house in a place called the Isle of Loch Morar, which seems to be the most proper place for the purpose in all this nation, considering my present circumstances, it being situated in the heart of our best and surest friends, where by boat all necessaries can be brought and all unnecessary distractions can be kept off. I have already got three or four boys together, which is perhaps more than I am able to maintain without some help. . . ."

When one compares the situation of the Morar Seminary with that in Glenlivet, which had fully as great disadvantages, one cannot but regret that the original

site was not retained in the case of the former as it was
in the case of the latter, which for nearly a hundred
years proved most useful to the mission in Scotland.
As Bishop McDonald remarks, Morar was the most
suitable site which he could find within his district.
The island is half-a-mile from the shore and of sufficient
size to provide a good garden and other ground for the
boys' exercise, while the distance from the shore is such
that they would be able to cross almost any day. The
island is, moreover, most picturesquely situated, and in
this has a great advantage over Scalan. No doubt it
was inconvenient to take all the stores over to the island,
but one cannot help thinking that if the chequered
history of the college in the future had been foreseen,
these inconveniences would have been borne with and
in time largely overcome. How long the boys actually
remained in "the large house" will be seen from
the subsequent pages to be doubtful; it was finally
abandoned after the Rising of 1745. Later Bishop
John MacDonald reopened the seminary at Buorblach,
a mile distant, but it did not prosper here either, and
at his death, in 1779, his successor transferred it to
Samalaman. Despite all the care and enthusiasm
bestowed on this foundation by Bishop Alexander
MacDonald, it was but little more successful, and Bishop
John Chisholm at once, upon his appointment as bishop,
sought a more desirable situation. In 1803 he removed
the seminary to Lismore, where it did fairly good work
until it was united with the Lowland seminary, and both
were transferred to Blairs College.

No doubt the difficulty regarding a site was largely
due to the unwillingness of the landlords to grant a lease

for the purpose; but everything seems to prove that if the college had been retained in the island on Loch Morar, this difficulty would never have arisen, while the island was large enough to be suitable for the eight or ten boys, which is all the college ever boasted until its removal to Blairs.

The plan of the college buildings can be traced on the island, whilst the walls of the garden are still standing, and enclose a fair amount of ground, of which the soil appears excellent. But to return to the early days of the foundation, Bishop McDonald writes to Mr Peter Grant, the new agent at Rome, in 1738: " I need not recommend to you to keep friends at Hambourg in mind of the promise they once made in the time of Mr Logan (Mr Stuart) of helping Mr Sandison's shop, which is now fixed in Arisaig. The number of prentices is eight, which is more than Mr Sandison would wish, but some of their parents were promising to help them, yet once they gott them off their hands, they never mind them. . . ." I could not reconcile the statement " which is now fixed in Arisaig " with the previous letters and with all the local traditions that the school was on Loch Morar. Certainly the Bishop's brother, the laird of Morar, lived at Bunacaimb, in Arisaig, and the Bishop might have used the term loosely. Since first writing the above, I have reread No. IV. of the papers following, from whence it appears that Bishop McDonald really did board his pupils with his brother at Arisaig. If the previous agreement had also been for five years, that would make it begin in 1737, and would account for the Bishop's expression in his letter of 1738, " is now fixed in Arisaig." The agreement of 1742 would still be

in force in 1745, and accounts for there being no mention
of a school on the island, when Bishop McDonald and his
companions were almost apprehended there.   From the
papers found it was evidently the residence of the Bishop,
but the whole account is best told in the words of the
contemporary account published in the *Scots Magazine*.

EXTRACT from a letter to the DUKE OF NEWCASTLE,
published in May, 1747.

"What has given rise to the present address is the
perusal of certain papers seized in the Macdonald's
country, in the North-west Highlands, by the Argyleshire militia.   The following circumstances I had from
the mouth of a gentleman who was a principal actor in
what he related ; to whom I am likewise indebted for
being allowed to take copies of the original papers seized.

"On the 8th June, 1746, Major-General Campbell
sailing with the bulk of his forces from Tobermory, in the
Isle of Mull, up Loch Sunart, the country of the Camerons
and other rebels, he detached Capt. Duff, of the Terror,
and Capt. Fergusson, of the Furnace, with several tenders,
to range and clear the coast of the more Westerly
Continent and Isles, and to look for the Pretender's
son, and other rebel chiefs ; as also to receive from the
common people their arms and ammunition.   For the
more effectual execution of these important services, the
General re-inforced them with a strong detachment of
Guise's and a few of Johnson's regiments of foot, commanded by Capt. James Miller ; together with two
Argyleshire companies, commanded by Capt. Dougall
Campbell, of Achachrosan, and Capt. Dougall Campbell,
of Cruachan.   They accordingly proceeded to Moydart and

Arisaig, where they found a great quantity of arms, and forty barrels of powder, hid amongst the rocks and woods.

" Having apprehended several of the rebels in those parts, they learned from them, that Lord Lovat, with his servants, and a guard of well-armed and resolute men, had retired into an island in Loch Morar, a fresh-water lake twelve miles in length, and somewhat more than a mile distant from the West sea-coast. In this pleasant little island, his Lordship lived with Macdonald of Morar, the proprietor of it, his brother Bishop Hugh Macdonald, the Pope's Apostolical Vicar of Scotland, one Dr Macdonald, and several others of that rebellious family. Here they deemed themselves perfectly secure, having for that end brought all the boats on the lake to their island ; never once suspecting the possibility of His Majesty's forces, being able to bring any boats from the sea, over land into this lake, to disturb their secure retreat. But they soon found themselves woefully mistaken ; for 300 men were quickly landed from the King's ships on that coast, under the command of Capt. Fergusson, and the two Captains Campbell before named, with the regular subalterns. These performed a most difficult and dangerous march of nine miles, from Arisaig to Loch Morar, over inconceivably rugged rocks, where oft-times but one man a-breast could clamber. Upon their arrival at the lake, they immediately spread themselves opposite to the isle, and in view of the rebels thereon ; who, concluding themselves quite free from danger, fired on our people, at the same time calling them by insulting and opprobrious names, being near enough to be heard. This exultation, however, was quickly at an end ; for the King's ships having sailed round to that part of the coast where their boats had little more than a mile to be carried overland to the lake (the brook that runs from the lake into the sea, near that place being too small for navigation) the rebels immediately lost all courage, upon observing the men-of-war's boats moving overland towards the lake and suddenly taking to their own boats, they rowed up the lake with the utmost precipitation; insomuch, that though the Argyleshire men swiftly pursued on both sides of the lake, and that our own boats followed as soon as they could be got into the lake, yet all the rebel gentry, Macdonalds, escaped into the mountains, excepting the before-named Dr Macdonald, whom our people apprehended, and brought back to the island, together with the boats of those rebels. Here they found the before-named Popish Bishop's house and chapel; which the sailors quickly gutted and demolished, merrily adorning themselves with the spoils of the chapel. In the scramble, a great many books and papers were tossed about and destroyed. One of the Argyleshire gentlemen, however, happened to get into his hands the few papers which have occasioned this address.

" Upon examining the prisoners, it was concluded, that Lord Lovat's lameness must have rendered it utterly impracticable for him to travel in so rugged a country, and that therefore he must probably lie concealed in one or other of the numberless caves at the upper end of this lake, where the boats had landed him. It was therefore determined to make diligent search every where thereabout. This service was performed by Capt. Fergusson, and other officers and men, with unwearied diligence, for three days and nights; when at length, Capt. Campbell

G

of Achachrosan found that unhappy Lord lying on two feather beds, not far from the side of the lake ; to whom he surrendered and delivered up his arms and strong box. Hereupon his Lordship was put into one of our boats and rowed down the lake, at the lower end of which our sailors MADE A RUN WITH HIM (as they termed it) over land to the sea-side, the pipers all the while playing the tune called Lord Lovat's march, with which his Lordship pretended to be pleased ; and finally they carried him on board Capt. Fergusson's ship."

Regarding the foregoing account, it evidently has not suffered in vividness in the telling, the object, of course, being to make the arrest appear as a gallant achievement ; though the capture of an old man of eighty needs " a rich brush " to give it any appearance of the kind. Bishop McDonald, it will be seen, managed to escape, and, after hiding in the neighbourhood as best he could, in autumn crossed over to France in one of the ships which had been sent to search for Prince Charlie. The Bishop went to Paris, and stayed some time at the Scots College, returning to Scotland in August, 1749.

The writer in the *Scots Magazine* then dwells on the dangerous nature of the papers—though indeed nothing more harmless could have been found, being, as they are, purely ecclesiastical orders and instructions. He also inveighs against " the country of the Camerons, Macdonalds, etc. It is amongst the worst of the people, many of whom are most cruel and barbarous thieves and murderers, as well as traitors, that the Pretender has his chief supporters." Unfortunately for the writer of the above, the whole campaign of Prince Charles Edward proved the chivalry and generosity of the little Highland army, whilst the robberies and murders which were perpetrated by its conquerors after Culloden pass all belief at the present date.

In the following paper the " Sovereign " is, of course, King James, whose letter requesting the appointment of Bishop McDonald will be found in the life of the latter (*Amer. Cath. Quart.*, October, 1915).

" No. 1 of papers found in the BISHOP'S house at Morar. BISHOP GORDON'S mandate to the Popish clergy and laity in the Highlands, dated the 29th October, 1731.

"TO ALL CHURCHMEN AND HONOURABLE CATHOLIC GENTLEMEN IN THE HIGHLANDS OF SCOTLAND.

" The Universal Pastor of the Catholick Church, considering maturely that my advanced years cannot allow me to serve you henceforth, as I have done for many years ; and that it will prove much for your advantage, and that of all the Highland countries in Scotland, to have a Bishop constantly to reside amongst you ; has, in his great wisdom, and tender love for you all, with the consent, and at the desire of our Sovereign, ordered the most worthy bearer, the most Reverend Hugh Macdonald, to be consecrated Bishop, to serve amongst you, as your chief Pastor and Bishop. And his Holiness sending him as Bishop, amongst you, appoints him also Vicar Apostolical with singular powers, to enable him to discharge this office with the greater honour and authority. Injoining you all to be ever obedient and submissive to this your Most Rev. Bishop, who also specially represents the Pope's person; and to execute all his orders and commands, assuring you that he will with his supreme authority support this your Most Rev. Bishop's authority and commands.   Threatening, at the same time, the most severe censures against any such as were so wicked as to be disobedient or refractory.   It belongs to me of duty, to intimate to you these most pious intentions of his Holiness, which he has made known to me; that, by honouring and obeying faithfully this your Most Rev. Bishop, you may show the more dutifully your reverence and respect to the supreme Pastor.

"Your exemplary obedience and submission to this your most honourable Pastor, will be a most assured means to draw down upon you all continually the special and most plentiful blessings of heaven; and will ever prove a most singular comfort to me, who have served you so long, and still retain such a tender love to you all in Christ.

JACOBUS

Ep. Nicop. Vic. Apost. in planis Scotiæ.

The second paper incidentally throws light on the position of the Catholic Church in the Highlands at this time.   It is noticeable that the meeting had been held again at Morar.   Bishop Hugh McDonald was not able to go to Rome, being probably unwilling to absent himself from his diocese for so long a period as the journey then required.   Accordingly Mr Tyrie and Mr Colin Campbell obtained permission to go by themselves. The journey was the beginning of much trouble, for the

" Pilgrims," as they came to be called, actually accused the Vicar Apostolic of the Lowland District, of Jansenism, and it took years for the bad impression to be put right.

" No. II. Instructions for Mr JOHN TYRIE, who, with the consent and approbation of his fellow Missionaries, in a meeting held at the Isle of Morar, in montanis, on the 14th and following days of April, 1735, was chosen by our most Rev. Bishop HUGH MACDONALD, Vicar Apostolic in montanis Scotiæ, to accompany him to the Old Town, in prosecution of the affairs spiritual and temporal of our Highland Mission.

[The writer in the *Scots Magazine* prefaces the following remarks :—" These instructions consist of twenty-one articles, many of which related purely to Tyrie's taking care of his bishop, both coming and returning : and concerning their own particular and separate interest as Highland Missionaries, as contra-distinguished from the Lowland Mission, who had a distinct bishop and Vicar Apostolic ; which last Mission the Highland Missionaries thought to be more favoured at Rome, in point of temporal concerns than they were. I shall therefore only exhibit such of the articles of these instructions as do more immediately relate to their propagation of Popery and disaffection in that country.]

" Art. V. The said Mr John Tyrie shall suggest to our Most Rev. Vicar while there [at Rome] the following motives for obtaining redress of our difficulties, both spiritual and temporal.

" That seeing we had no subjects from Paris College, for above twenty years past ; nor did the Superior thereof call for youths from our Highlands, for upwards of fifteen years past ; therefore all possible means shall be used with our great friend [King James III.] to concur with our Most Rev. Vicar, in procuring such a reformation of that house, as to render it more useful in time to come to the Highland Mission. For effectuating of this that it be represented to our said great friend, how all his best friends here are interested in the good of this Mission ; and that the increase of Catholicks here will much advance his own interest ; that nothing will be more agreeable to them, than that the same house educate their children, as it does those of the Low country [of Scotland].

" Art. VII. For obtaining what we desire, in this point, from our great friend, it is ordered, that the letters formerly sent by both Vicars Apostolical and some of their clergy then present, be presented to him, if they can be had, otherwise the copies of the said letters which are here.

" Art. VIII. That the said Mr John Tyrie carry along with him a copy of the catechism reprinted with additions ; and mind our Most Rev. Vicar to lay it before the persons concerned there, to have their judgment upon the same.

" Art. IX. For obtaining assistance from Propaganda in our wants, that it be represented, that if we had necessary charges, we could, under God, make considerable conversions in the country about us.

" Art. X. That the Propaganda be informed of the methods that the enemies of the truth fall on for extirpating it ; such as, the charity schools founded on purpose to entice and imbibe youth with bad principles ; the yearly pensions bestowed for maintaining itinerant preachers among our people ; the erecting of new Parish Ministers in such places where our folks mostly prevail in number. And all these three foundations are principally designed against our Highland countries. Nor must it be forgot to represent, that the £1,000 Sterling allowed by King George to itinerant Ministers in the Highlands, is in a great part employed in perverting Catholics. That our parts, generally speaking, have an inclination to the faith, all our chief heads of families no ways hindering their followers. That all this be laid before our great friend, as a motive to gain him over to our interest.

" Art. XI. That our present number of Missionaries being but eleven, and our Catholicks so situated in their contiguous isles and small villages, that one Missionary can serve but very few totally well, we absolutely have need of double the number we have at present, with subsistence for them. The Propaganda then must be supplicated to afford both the one and the other.

" Art. XII. That though both Colleges [the Scots Colleges of Rome and Paris] were rendered as useful for our purpose as they are capable of, yet still we should want many of the necessary number of missionaries ; and even if we got two thirds of both colleges, yet they would not be a proportion to the number of Catholicks in the Highlands.

" Art. XV. That our Most Rev. Vicar, out of his zeal for religion, and for the good of the souls under his care, has, out of his small funds, begun a seminary in our Highlands. Therefore the Propaganda is to be supplicated to grant to our Most Rev. Vicar such charitable assistance as shall render him capable to prosecute his most pious design : without which he must necessarily drop it.

"I John Tyrie do solemnly swear and vow, that I shall faithfully and diligently concur, by the grace of God, with my worthy Most Rev. Vicar Apostolical in all his affairs ; and with the like fidelity and diligence, shall discharge the trust committed to me, by my fellow Missionaries, according to the tenor of their above signed instructions given me. So help me God and this his holy Gospel.

"JOANNES TYRIUS,

"*Presb. in Mont. Scotiæ.*

"We under subscribers attest this to be a true copy of the original.

"NILE M'FIE	JOHN M'DONALD
"JAM. GRANT, *Writer*	COLIN CAMPBELL
"ÆNEAS M'LACHLAN	JOHN TYRIE."

The next paper gives the list of the Catholic clergy in Scotland at this time. Regarding the Highland priests, the lives of most of those mentioned can now be pieced together, though the last-named seems to have been a Franciscan, and only appears in the list for this year. Henderson is an *alias* for Harrison.

"III. A list of the Popish missionaries in the Lowlands
and Highlands of Scotland, as they stood *anno*
1740.

Alex. Drummond	Æneas M'Lachlan
Alex. Paterson	John M'Donald
—— Hackett	Colin Campbell
Robert Gordon	Nile M'Fie
William Shand	James Leslie
John Tyrie	James Grant
John Godsman	Francis M'Donald
George Gordon	W. Henderson
Alexander Gordon	—— O'Kelly
John Gordon	—— O'Colgan "
George Duncan	
William Duthie	
Charles Crookshank	
William Reid	

The fourth paper is, unfortunately, not given in its
original form. I can only give the remarks of the
Scots Magazine writer regarding it :

" IV. is a further proof of their great industry for the
promoting of their cause. It contains articles of agreement, dated the 1st May 1742, betwixt the before-named
Bishop Macdonald, and his brother John Macdonald,
for the latter to board and maintain five boys and a
master to teach them. This Popish seminary was to
continue for five years certain ; and probably may be
still in being, and farther prolonged, unless speedy and
effectual means be used for clearing the country of such
poisonous weeds "

The last of the papers in the *Scots Magazine*

as being found at Morar is the cypher commonly used by the bishops and clergy of that period. I insert it by itself, omitting the comments of the *Scots Magazine*:

" The Cypher	The Key
Hambourg	Rome
West	Highlands
Amsterdam	Paris
Grisly's shop	Scots College, Paris
Hambourg shop	Scots College, Rome
Mr Cant	The Pope
The Change	The College of Propaganda
Mr Arthur	The King (James)
Merchant	Cardinal
Physician	Bishop
Labourers	Clergy
Birly	Jesuit
Mr James Grant	Bishop Gordon
Grigson	Mr Cowreyer
Melvill	Mr Thomas
Mr Debree	Mr Innes "

Of the youths educated at Morar it is difficult to form even a rough list, though the names of a few occur in the letters of the Bishops. Mr Allan Macdonald taught there for some years after his ordination in 1736, and from his not being included in List No. IV. I infer that he was then teaching, and not on the active mission. He accompanied Prince Charlie, was apprehended, and kept for eight months on a hulk in the Thames, and six months longer in Newgate. He died in 1781, and left such money as he had saved to the Highland Seminary.

But by this time the little establishment had moved to Buorblach.

Bishop John MacDonald was appointed coadjutor to his uncle in 1761. He at once recommenced the project of a Highland school, which had been in abeyance since 1746. He had it in working order in 1767, according to the following letter of Bishop Hugh :—" . . . the keeping of boys at Fochabers has been very chargeable to me and they are not so well taught as I would like ; I have now begun a new shop in the West under the direction of Mr Tiberiop. ; and Mr Allen (jun.) one of the travellers lately come, is to be constantly with the apprentices to teach them. By this I expect to have subjects better prepared than formerly, at least in a short time. It's true I may meet with difficulties and the want of funds is a great one ; however I shall do my best and depend on Providence."

But the situation at Buorblach was not entirely to the liking of Bishop Hugh. He had been all his life in such straitened circumstances as did not admit of hospitality ; hence he writes to Bishop Hay, 10th October 1769 : " In short the shop in the West does not answer my expectations, for I could keep boys at Fochabers much cheaper than there. The reason is that Mr John's house is full of comers and goers every night, and what should be spent on boys is spent on stragglers. This gives me great uneasiness, and I am by time to bring the boys back to Fochabers."

We learn something of these youths from a letter of Bishop John to Bishop Hay, written from North Morar, 20th August 1770 : " I cannot give the same assurance of the number you ask of prentices, for one of them is doubtful, who is indeed the least hopeful of the six we had. But the rest shall be ready at a call, viz. Austin MacDonald from South Uist, Son to Alex. MacDonald and Margaret MacEachan of Morar's family; Donald MacDonell, son to John MacDonell brother to Mr Alexander junr. and Margaret MacDonald niece to Mr Dian (Bishop Hugh M'Donald). Angus MacDonald from Braelochaber, son to James MacDonald of Keppoch's family and his mother of the Stewarts of Appin, a very good convert. Duncan MacDonald also from Braelochaber, whose parents are not yet Catholics, but his father, of Keppoch's family, is soon expected to become one. His mother is Grant from Strathspey; and finally Donald MacDonald son to Ranald MacDonald uncle to Kinlochmoydart and Margery MacDonald sister to the late Mr Æneas MacDonald who died at Barry. The readiest means of providing the sixth is to call from Glenlivet the son of one Lachlan MacDonald there recommended last year." Of the above Austin MacDonald and Angus certainly persevered and became useful missionaries in the Highlands.

Bishop John MacDonald put his whole heart and soul into the new foundation, as appears from a letter of Bishop Hugh to his brother bishop in Edinburgh: "Mr Tibcriop. is continually making up houses on his new farm. The charges are great for I have given him no less than £74 which indeed I would not be able to give, had I not been pretty well provided beforehand, and I hope he will not make any demand in haste; if he does, I know not what to say or do. I fear he is much for projects, and what gives me great trouble is that the boys are not kept to their lessons."

The younger bishop had now taken over most of the work of the vicariate from his uncle, and to his worries regarding the school was added the difficulty of supplying priests to the various districts. Bishop Hugh writes in August, 1772: "Mr Tiberiop has been with me for eight days not long since. He is greatly harassed for want of Missionaries." The same subject is referred to in the Annual Letter of the Bishops for 1774: "Tiberiop. is in such difficulties that he cannot take up his residence in any one district. He is often at a loss to know which district to attend to first, so urgent and so frequent are the calls that are made upon him. Even if he could comply with all the requests he could not afford them much permanent help. It was with much regret and with great injury to religion that he was forced to close the little seminary which he had started a few years previously. He could however not possibly spare any one to attend to it."

Although the good Bishop writes from Buorblach in January, 1775, he had apparently no pupils with him at that time. After stating that he was very uncertain where to settle, but preferred Buorblach, he continues: "I cannot help regretting that Scalans cannot be joined. . . . If I set up a shop next year, I'll need a cargo of books for it." There was also the question of securing a lease, as to which he writes to Bishop Hay: "I got indeed an abatement of rent, but no lease, which made me soon repent of not quitting it" And again: "In case I go there I shall expect to return by Braemar, by this country and Strathglass, which will employ me all summer, and in autumn I would need to visit the Isles, after which I shall endeavour to settle myself for the winter season in some place, perhaps at Buorblach, which if I can get a lease of,[1] I would make my residence. I find myself considerably impaired by the many inconveniences of wandering without a fixed home, and cannot longer continue."

By the beginning of 1777, Bishop John had started the school afresh, for in February of that year he writes for his "cargo of books," and names the following :—

Rudiman's Rudiments . . .	3 copies
Cornelius, without translation .	7 copies
Cæsar	4 copies
Mair's Introduction to Making Latin	3 copies
Ovid de Fastis	2 copies
Rudiman's Grammar . . .	3 copies
Cicero's Select Epistles . . .	5 copies
Cicero (Offices)	4 copies
Virgil	2 copies

The new beginning seemed to prosper little better than the previous one. Certainly a more distressing letter than the following could scarcely have been written. After stating that he is greatly concerned at the proposal to sell Buorblach over his head, he most earnestly begs that the Mission funds be used to purchase the whole for £2,000. "For a sinking Fund to relieve me of this burden I shall assign my Scalan funds and every penny I can spare from my own subsistence. Even if it should be necessary to dismiss my Scalan entirely for 7 or 8 years, and take boys to be sent to the shops, the best way I could find them, I would rather do it than lose this

[1] I was told locally that it was Macdonald, of Girinish, in Uist, who made difficulties about granting a lease, and that he was the cause of the college being later moved to another district.

opportunity. However my economy may have been, which had no other fault, but too easily burdening myself to relieve others, you may assure yourself, I shall readily —for securing the point—reduce myself to mere necessaries of life. For of all temporal things, it lies nearest to my heart; and failing in this attempt will be the greatest mortification of my life."

Bishop John MacDonald seems to have been one of those men who could refuse no call upon his charity. He is often stated, by the other bishops, as trying to fill the place of two and even three of his priests. He had also burdened himself with debt to relieve the distress of his people. In October, 1777, he writes from Buorblach to the Cardinal Prefect of Propaganda:

" The reason why I was not at the meeting of Bishops this year was that circumstances obliged me in the month of June to go to the Western Islands to administer Confirmation which had already been too long delayed. The journey, which is one of 60 miles across dangerous seas, can never be made with any comfort except in summer, nor is one sure of getting back if one goes at other times. When I had finished my work and was ready to return, I was detained by contrary winds, and did not reach the mainland until the beginning of September. By that time my Colleagues had dispersed, whilst even if they had still been at the Meeting I could not have gone there, so stormy and wet was the weather. At once on my arrival here I wrote to Bishop Hay, to learn what they had settled and I soon after received his reply. I then started to write to your Eminence, but I was taken seriously ill and was thereafter so weak that any reading or writing was almost impossible to me.

I only mention this here, to account for my delay in writing to your Eminence."

In the same letter the Bishop goes on to say : " Mr James MacDonald, who seven years ago came from the Scots College, Paris, is to help the priest in Knoydart. He is of strong constitution and will be a great help to his two neighbours. For two years he had charge of the seminary when we began it in this district. He is succeeded by Mr Austin MacDonald, who returned in poor health from Valladolid, when only in deacon's orders, and who will now prepare himself for the priesthood and preside over the boys in the seminary." This Austin MacDonald I take to be the same who passed through Buorblach and was stated to be ready to go to the Colleges abroad in 1770.

Bishop John MacDonald attended the meeting of Bishops at Scalan in 1778, and their Annual Letter breathes a spirit of hope and of progress which must have been a great encouragement to the good bishop in his personal difficulties. They say : " Regarding the present state of affairs, we were never more hopeful, never more prosperous, and we trust that all our hopes will shortly be realised. The road is much easier for converts, and many difficulties which heretofore hindered them are about to be removed. The liberality of the King and of the Ministry gives us great hopes for the future, and we already enjoy far greater liberty than ever our forefathers had."

This was destined to be the last Annual Letter of Bishop John MacDonald In the following spring, whilst staying in Knoydart, he caught an epidemic then raging there, and in five days he passed to a better world. We have

seen that he was in bad health two years previously—
indeed his health had been undermined by the fatigues
and labours of his missionary life and he fell an easy
prey to the infection, caught at the death-bed of a
parishioner. He was buried in Kilchoan Cemetery,
Knoydart.

The life work of this excellent man is best judged from
the letters of the time, which almost invariably refer to
him as " good Bishop John," and Bishop Hay greatly
regretted his loss as a colleague. He heartily sym-
pathised with his priests in their life of labour and
fatigue, and during the eighteen years of his episcopate
was unremitting in his endeavours to relieve them. In
this manner he was himself worn out at the early age
of fifty-two. His successor, Bishop Alexander MacDonald,
at once began to look for a more suitable site for the
seminary, and in 1783 it was again removed from the
Morar district to Samalaman, in Moydart.

Regarding the succession of priests in this district,
Mr James Hugh MacDonald was here in 1779, for, in the
election of a successor to Bishop John, he signs as Priest
of Morar. From that date onward the succession is given
in the parish Register as follows :—

" The Rev. Reginald M'Donell came to the Mission of
North Morar in 1782, and laboured for 50 years in the
same Mission. In 1832 he was succeeded by Rev. Coll
M'Coll, who laboured in the same Mission for 10 years.
The Rev. Donald M'Kay took charge of the Mission of
N. Morar in 1842 and spent 28 anxious years at Bracara.
The Rev. Donald M'Innes succeeded in the year 1870,
and held the charge till 17th Dec. 1873. The Rev.
Donald Walker had charge of the North Morar Mission

H

till Dec. 1888. He was succeeded by Rev. Donald M'Lellan, until the death of the latter in 1903. Rev. James Chisholm had charge for six months, and Rev. Angus Macrae from 1904 onward."

At Morar chapel-house is preserved a set of green vestments, with red and white intermingled, bearing the date 1745. It still has its original lining; there is also an altar frontal to match it These were probably brought over from France by the adherents of Prince Charlie, and must have been part of the furnishings of the chapel on the island, though it is not known how they were saved when the building was ransacked and burnt in 1746. The same remarks apply to the old chalice, which bears the inscription: " Ad usum Pr Fr Vincentii Mariani, Missrii Scot. Ord. Praedic. Anno 1658." This chalice, which is of silver, is very small indeed; it has its paten to match. Unfortunately we have no further information regarding this early missioner. In the list of priests for 1668 it is stated that there were three Dominicans on the mission. Father Vincent was apparently one of these; the others being Father George Fanning— long in the Isle of Barra—and Father Primrose, who died in prison in 1671.

Of the priests above mentioned Mr Reginald M'Donell had, according to Bishop Alexander MacDonald's Report for the year 1783, 250 Catholics in South Morar and 460 in North Morar, besides 46 in the Loch Arkaig district. " In 1822 he had been 40 years in this Mission," writes Bishop Ranald MacDonald, " and was then sixty-six years of age."

Mr Ronald (Reginald) M'Donell had no house of his own, but, according to the custom of the time, stayed one

CHURCH OF ST CUMIN, LOCH MORAR

To face page 115

week in one house, a second week in another, and so on, from the end of Loch Nevis to Mallaig. His mother was not a Catholic, and was unkind to the boy, especially after her second marriage; but he had the happiness of receiving her into the Church on her death-bed. It is still remembered how at one time there were three ministers in the sick-room, but one after the other they went away, and so left the priest alone with his mother, for whose reception into the Church he had long and earnestly prayed.

When Mr Ronald was already advanced in years, Mr Coll M'Coll was sent to assist him. Mr M'Coll was from Tyree, and was thirty years of age before he was converted. " He was a great boy for the fiddle and was oh so greatly loved; but in consequence of an accusation against him he had to go to Australia—the woman who made the accusation lost her arm—it went bad and her cries could be heard five miles away."

The older chapel was at Bracora, and this was succeeded by the one at present standing, which was built in 1836: towards its erection T. A. Fraser, Esq. —grandfather of the present Lord Lovat—contributed £100, so runs the Directory of that date. In 1889 it was superseded by the present very pretty chapel at Beoraid, erected entirely at the cost of the Lovat family, in memory of Simon, Lord Lovat, who had a special affection for the Morar portion of his property, and who often stayed for long periods together at Morar Lodge, the great beauty of its surroundings having a special attraction for him. Mass is still sometimes said at Bracora, and the school continues to be conducted there, whilst there are few churches in the Highlands which are better filled than the church of St Cumin at Morar. On the Sundays when the present writer was there, it was a most picturesque sight to see the keepers and gillies coming down Loch Morar in their boats, while the road, eastwards from Bracora and westwards from Mallaig, was crowded with people. One can but hope that his ancient mission may long flourish, and that its people will remember how two hundred years ago, Morar was the centre of Catholic life in the Highlands of Scotland, and how so entirely Catholic was it that they still boast: " There was never a minister's sermon in this country until the railway came "—as recently as 1890.

ARISAIG

MR ALEXANDER LESLIE, whose Report I have already had occasion to quote, mentions that at the time of his Visitation in 1678 the people of Arisaig had just lost their priest, Mr George Fanning, an Irish Dominican. " For this reason when the people saw Mr Munro, they thought that they were the objects of the special grace of Heaven, thinking that he had come to labour amongst them. But when they heard that we were to go in three days to the Outer Isles their joy was turned to bitter disappointment, and they loudly complained that they were neglected and abandoned by the priests." How long Father George Fanning had been with them, we do not know, but in 1671 he was in Barra, and had been there some years at that date. I presume that he is buried at Kilmorui in Arisaig, in the cemetery which is so full of memories, both pre-Reformation and of later date.

This complaint of the people of Arisaig that they were abandoned by the priests is constantly repeated throughout the Highland districts at this period. In 1664 Mr Francis White had written to St Vincent of Paul: " I send you this to let you know that the great burden which I bear has made me break down and has placed me 'hors de combat.' You indeed know how much work I had when four other priests helped me, now that I am alone in this Mission, pray tell me how I can possibly keep up, especially as I have converted as many more of

117

these poor people, who show themselves daily better disposed for instruction and the Sacraments. Such a work cannot be carried on by one poor workman, weak and infirm as I am. Indeed you know it has almost cost me my life. I have 4,000 souls to assist,[1] and these too dispersed in different districts in the Isles, and other remote places. If only I had help I would hope to convert many more, but against my will I am forced to leave off making new converts, not being able to serve more than once in two years, those I have already converted, whilst there are remote islands, which I have not visited for three years."

Again, in 1665, Mr Francis White wrote : " If I could have three or four Irish priests, I would sooner have them than twenty others, but they must be good men, otherwise I would sooner have no assistance at all. . . . If your Reverence [St Vincent of Paul] has not any Irish priests at hand, you might write to the Superior of the Scots College, Paris, who could find many in that University ; and even if all are not fit for this most laborious Mission, assuredly from amongst so many, a selection could be made, and the best be sent. I say this for the discharge of my conscience. . . ."

So urgent an appeal could not fail to impress Propaganda, which at once ordered that all the recommendations of Father White be carried into effect. The Nuncio at Paris was instructed to order John White, brother of Father Francis, to go to the assistance of this latter. The Archbishop of Armagh was asked to find priests in Ireland who knew the Celtic language and were willing to labour in the Highlands ; the General of the Jesuits was asked

---

[1] Certainly a very low estimate —F O B.

to find suitable youths to go to the National Colleges, of which visitations were to be made by the different Nuncios, who were asked to send in full reports to Propaganda.

This same subject of the scarcity of priests was later a constant source of anxiety to the Vicars Apostolic. Bishop Gordon writes, in 1711, to the agent in Rome: " I have extreme difficulty in getting these countries served with labourers, though I leave no stone unturned to get some. Mr M'Gregor stayed with us but a few months, and is returned to Germany again. . . . I have great difficulty in keeping the labourer I brought home with me, who is one of the usefullest, though he does not please me so well as at first. I strive to make the few labourers we have the most useful I can to these countries. . . " Again, a few years later, he wrote: " We cannot without deep regret travel through whole districts and see so many souls perishing who would readily embrace the Faith, if only we had priests who could reside amongst them, to teach and instruct them."

Later still, in 1732, Bishop Hugh McDonald, after his first journey through the Highlands as their Vicar Apostolic, writes: " Wide tracts of country which have of necessity been assigned to single priests on account of the scarcity of these, far exceed the capacity of the most diligent worker. . . . The faithful greatly lament the scarcity of priests and grieve that while those in other parts enjoy all spiritual comforts, they themselves suffer the greatest need, not from any want of zeal on the part of the labourers, but from their scarcity."

One more quotation on this subject, and that the most striking, from the pen of good Bishop Hugh McDonald again, I cannot refrain from adding : " The few labourers we have are so tired with troubles, that some of them are threatening to forsaick the Western trade, but if any more follow the example of those who have already left us, you may expect to hear that Mr Sandison [Bishop Hugh himself—son of Sandy M'Donald] has doon the same, for it's impossible for him to stand out alone."

But to return to an earlier date, Mr Morgan was priest in Arisaig in 1700, at the time of Bishop Nicolson's Visitation. Mr Morgan had then been thirteen years in the Highland mission, but in June of the following year he was apprehended in Arisaig, was imprisoned, and banished from the country. From the fact that Bishop Nicolson took him as his interpreter on his journey through the Isles, we can surmise that he was a man of solid piety and learning. Bishop Nicolson had arrived at Keppoch in Arisaig, on 15th June 1700. Here he found a Catholic school. Arisaig is described as " less hilly and more pleasant than Knoydart, Morar or Moydart, which are all much the same in regard to rock and mountains—whilst Arisaig is much more level and abounds in corn. The Chief of Clanranald, being by chance on the mainland, came to receive the Bishop with great kindness and courtesy, and placed at his disposal one of his boats with most experienced sailors to take him wherever he wished in the Islands."

The Report of the Visitation has some interesting archæological notes, which are here given *verbatim*. " Kilmarui, *i.e.* the Cell or Church of St Malrubber, is close to Keppoch in Arisaig. In this chapel there are several tombs of a hard bluish stone, on which there are some ancient figures very well carved, but without

inscription for the most part. One would not have thought
that the people of these countries had as much skill in
sculpture as these tombs show them to have had. There
are some on which a priest, wearing the ancient form of
chasuble, is engraved; others have only figures of arms,
such as large swords, or else figures of birds and other
animals. There are similar tombs on Eilean Finnan
(where the lairds of Moydart are buried), in Eigg, in Uist,
Barra, and in several other islands off the North of
Scotland. In this respect Icolmkill, anciently called Hy,
is very noteworthy. Here was the celebrated Abbey, of
which Bede speaks in several places, founded by St
Columba, Abbot and Doctor, and Apostle of part of
Scotland. This Abbey was held in the greatest veneration until the so-called Reformation, when it was pillaged
and destroyed. The tombs of the ancient kings of Scotland, and of all the chief families in the Highlands were
here, and the Highlanders think with considerable prob-
ability that after the decadence of religion, when the Abbey
had been profaned and ruined, the chiefs each brought
back to the churches on their own lands some of the
tombs of their fore-fathers. I also saw two stone crosses,
well carved with strange figures; one in the cemetery of
St Columba, in the Isle of Canna, and the other at
Kilchoan (i.e. Church of St Colgan), in Knoydart, where
is the burial place of the lairds of that country."

There is much of interest in this Report of Bishop
Nicolson; for example, after stating that many most
ancient customs survive amongst the Highlanders, he
continues: "They are divided into clans each under its
own Chief. They have a great care of their genealogies,
and the Lairds have genealogists from father to son,

who write what concerns the clan. They are much given to following the military profession ; their character, the roughness of their land, and their manner of life render them well suited to it. There is not the humblest peasant but has his sword, his musket, his targe and a large dirk, which is always to be seen hanging at his side. Besides these arms the gentry use helmets and breastplates. By nature they are of very lively spirits and they are wonderfully successful when they have a little education. Even the common people seem to be far more open and confiding than those of the Lowlands. Indeed, what makes them seem to be less so, when they first come amongst strangers, is their want of experience, and their ignorance of a language and of customs different from their own.

"It is not my place," continues the writer of the Report, "to describe here all those customs of theirs which differ from ours, consisting as they do in their manner of life, of dress, etc. Suffice it to say that they feed very coarsely, never eat more than twice at most in the day, use over their short dress a plaid which also serves them as a covering at night, whilst their bedding is very hard. This, however, does not apply to persons of rank, who in their food and clothing often enough follow the customs of civilised countries. Nor does it apply to the Islesmen, who dress in the manner of the Lowlanders when they are at home, but when they go out on any expedition they wear Highland dress. The costume of the women seems to us even more extraordinary, for they wear the plaid girded like the men except that the plaid reaches to the ground and is fastened in front of the breast with a brooch of copper."

The Report then repeats the statement regarding the attachment of the Highlanders to their ancient customs and their dislike of novelties. The arable land is stated to be of small extent, but to give a good return, and that with little labour. Snow lies but a short time in the sea-board districts and in the Isles. The horses and the flocks, which are very numerous, are outside all the winter, exposed to the weather night and day. Stables and byres they have none, except the gentry, who have stables for their saddle horses. It continues: "All these districts are very difficult to reach except by sea, on account of the mountains and cliffs which surround them. It is only strangers, however, and those un-accustomed to the hills who have any great difficulty in travelling through them, for the inhabitants themselves have little difficulty. It is an extraordinary thing that they prefer to go forty miles, for example, always climbing up and down, and are less tired thus, than if they had to go the same distance on a level road, where there was neither hill nor dale."

I have had occasion to quote this Report, when dealing with other districts, but here insert other portions of it, both previous to the arrival of the Bishop of Arisaig and after his departure thence for the Isles. No doubt the incident mentioned in the Report that Clanranald placed his best boat at the disposal of the Bishop accounts for the fact that it was from Arisaig that he sailed for the Hebrides, and returned there again after the Visitation. Clanranald would then be staying at Glen House, near Loch nan Eala. The house is now a quarter of a mile from the loch, but in those days it was at the water's edge, for the story goes that at least one chief used to fish from the window of his house in the waters of Loch nan Eala.

" We started from the Enzie, in Banffshire, on 24th May, 1700, going by boat, in order to attract less notice, and in order to avoid passing through Moray and Inverness. There was a strong wind in our favour, so that we soon covered the sixty miles ; but as the tide, which is very strong here, was against us, we were terribly tossed about between the force of the wind, and of the tide, and were in great danger. At midnight we arrived at a friendly house, the Castle of Lovat (Note IV), six miles from Inverness. The next day the Bishop, who had been very seasick, took a rest, and I went into the town to call upon an excellent lady, the widow of the late Lord Macdonald. This nobleman had contributed more than any one else to bring back the Highlands and Islands to the Faith, being, as he was, one of the most important men in the Highlands and full of zeal. Close to Lovat Castle and on the banks of the river is Beauly Abbey, of which the Abbot's house is almost entire, along with the ruins of the cloister and a rather fine church."

On 27th May the Bishop and his party arrived in Strathglass, which is described as twelve miles from Lovat. He greatly admired the valley of the Glass river, one of the most beautiful in all Scotland, with its fine arable land along the river-side and the wooded hills rising on either bank. Timber was then in such abundance that all the houses were built of it. " They are called Creil houses, because the larger timbers are interlaced with wickerwork in the same way that baskets are made. They are covered outside with sods, or divots. All the houses on the mainland, wherever we went, are built after this fashion, except those of the lairds and principal gentry. Strathglass is partly inhabited by Frasers, whose chief is Lord Lovat, and partly by Chisholms under the Laird of Strathglass These latter are all Catholics."

The Bishop and his party next visited Glengarry, the distance of which from Strathglass they calculated at twenty-three miles, but each of these they thought as bad as a league and more. They had horses to carry the baggage, but the Bishop was obliged to go on foot most of the time, especially amongst the rocks and boulders, where it was often necessary to creep on hands and feet, and in the swamps, which were almost continuous. The account goes on : " Our ordinary lodgings on the journey were the shielings, or little cabins of earth four or five feet broad and six feet long, into which one enters by crouching on the ground, nor can one stand upright when arrived inside. These shielings the Highlanders use as shelters in the hills and forests, where they pasture their flocks, as also to store their dairy produce. In the Braes of Glengarry we were met by some gentlemen of the district, a few of whom were confirmed as secretly as possible, because the garrison, which occupied the castle of the Chief, was not far off."

The Bishop stayed only one day in Glengarry, leaving word with the priest to have the people ready for Confirmation against his return. This he was obliged to do in the other districts also that he traversed, for he was in a great hurry to reach the Isles as soon as possible. He had been informed that the seas which he had to cross were very dangerous, and indeed even to-day, with a good steamboat service, the journey is not lightly to be undertaken. The description of the seas is quite accurate :

"We knew that they were very dangerous, not only because they form part of the vast ocean, but more especially because of the different currents, several of which one sometimes encounters at the same time, each contrary to the other, and these beat up against each other with tremendous force. It is thus only during three months of the year that one can cross to these distant islands in safety in the open boats, which are the only ones in that country."

After visiting the Islands of Eigg, Canna, Uist, Barra and Rum, the Bishop and his party got back to Arisaig on the mainland, on 29th July. "After our return from the Isles," the Report continues, "we began the Visitation of Arisaig, Moydart and Morar, and in the eight stations in this neighbourhood 700 persons were confirmed. Next day we drew up rules for the Catholic school which is in Arisaig, and then we went to Eilean Ban, in Morar, where we met the neighbouring missioners, and after consultation with them we drew up some disciplinary regulations. . . .

"On 29th September we returned to our starting point after a journey of over 400 miles. During the whole three months that the Visitation lasted the Bishop worked so hard that there were only three days, according to a careful diary that he kept, when he was not engaged from morning till night, either travelling from place to place, or preaching, confirming and catechising the people. Although he gave Confirmation almost every day, still it was his invariable custom never to do so without preaching himself as a preparation. His words were at once interpreted to the people by one of his suite. He scarcely gave himself a moment's repose, notwithstanding the very great fatigue of so difficult a journey."

Of the priests who successively served the mission of Arisaig, Mr Alexander MacDonald, "a man who loved fatigue," had charge of both Arisaig and Moydart in 1763. He was still there in 1779, for in the election of Bishop Alexander MacDonald he signs as "Alexander MacDonald, Provicarius, Miss. in Arisaig." In 1782 he writes from Arisaig to Propaganda, stating that he had then been thirty-five years on the Highland Mission, having left the Scots College, Rome, in 1747. He died in Arisaig, 13th March 1797, aged seventy-eight, having at that time just completed fifty years of missionary life, of which the greater part had been spent in this district.

In 1777 Mr James MacDonald had been appointed to assist the foregoing and another Alexander MacDonald, then priest of Knoydart, but how long he remained I have not ascertained. Between the years 1798 and 1801 Mr Evan Maceachan and Mr Charles MacDonald were stationed in Arisaig for short periods. The latter returned to Borrodale in his old age, and he there breathed his last, after an illness of only a few days, on 6th October 1848. He is interred at Kilmorrie, in Arisaig.

Mr John Macdonald was the next priest, and he remained in Arisaig till his death, in 1834, having thus completed at least thirty years in this mission. In 1822 Bishop Ranald MacDonald reports to Propaganda: "Separated from Moydart by high mountains and by an arm of the sea, is the district of Arisaig, partly high ground and partly cultivated. It is almost entirely Catholic, and until recently contained more than 1,000 people, but a few years ago about 300 emigrated. Here

Mr John Macdonald is priest, a man full of fervour, a student, and later Professor at Valladolid. He is now 67 years of age." His obituary notice gives some further details: "At Rinaleoid, in Arisaig, died Rev. John Macdonald, aged 82. Having at an early age been sent to the Seminary of Buorblach, which was then conducted by Rev. John Macdonald—afterwards Bishop—he was there converted to the Catholic Faith, and went about 1778 to the Scots College, Valladolid. He there remained several years, partly as student and later as professor. He came to Scotland in 1782 and was sent to Moydart, where he remained but a short period. From Moydart he was transferred to Barra, and having continued there for a few years, he was appointed to the charge of Arisaig, as successor to Rev. Alexander Macdonald, of the Kinlochmoydart family. In this Mission he died, 8th July, 1834, and is buried at Kilmorui.

"The next priest also was stationed at Arisaig for nearly forty years. Mr William Mackintosh was born in Glenmuick in 1794. In his youth he was renowned for his great physical powers and intrepidity, no less than for his straightforward manly disposition. He entered Lismore in 1821, when grown to man's estate. From 1826 to 1830 he was at St Sulpice, where he was ordained in 1831. He was in Barra from 1835 to 1837, and went from there to Arisaig, where he was destined to labour for the long period of forty years, loved and venerated by his flock, and respected by all with whom he came in contact. The Congregation at that time numbered 1,400. There was urgent need of a new church, as the one used by the Catholics was both

ST MARY'S, ARISAIG

With Ruins of pre-Reformation Church

To face page 120

unfinished and unsuitable in other respects. Mr Mackintosh applied himself vigorously to supply the want. He travelled through part of Great Britain and Ireland in 1845; and with the funds he collected he was enabled to build a large and handsome church, which was solemnly opened by Bishop Murdoch in 1849. Later on he added a school-house and teacher's residence, and in 1874 built a small chapel in the Braes of Arisaig, where Mass is still said once a month. He was a man of apostolic simplicity of habits, living upon the plainest fare, and whilst he was hospitable in the extreme, he spent very little upon his own comforts. Such was the reliance placed in his judgment and prudence that he was frequently consulted by the various bishops who successively ruled the Western District of Scotland, on matters appertaining to the Highlands, and for some time he held the position of Vicar-General of the Western Highlands " (Cath. Direct. 1878). [1]

Of the great work accomplished by Mr Mackintosh little more need be said here. The Catholic church of Arisaig will ever be his monument. Its situation, facing the sea, and well above the town, is very striking. Less well known is the little church in the Braes of Arisaig, yet I well remember the Sunday when I visited it. It was a beautiful October morning, and the scenery down Loch Ailort on the one side, and towards Arisaig on the other, was very striking. The congregation soon filled the little church, and of all the Highland churches I have visited—and I have had the pleasure

---

[1] "The Old Vicar," as the late Bishop Angus Macdonald used to call him, lived all his time in Keppoch Farm House, which is still standing. He was tenant of the farm.

I

of saying Mass in most of them—the little church in the Braes of Arisaig has for me the pleasantest recollections.

Another most worthy son of Catholic Arisaig, though indeed he did not labour long within the district of his birth, was Mr Evan Maceachan, "who descended full of years and merits to the grave" in 1849, and had been born in Arisaig in 1769. When eleven years of age he left the Highlands, along with his parents, and was sent to school near Huntly. In 1788 he repaired to the Scots College, Valladolid, where he became remarkable for earnest application to study. He was ordained priest at Valladolid in 1798. He did not at once, however, return to the Scotch Mission, but assisted Bishop Cameron during two years in the discharge of the episcopal duties of that diocese, at the request of the Bishop of Valladolid who was then aged and infirm.

On his return to his native country, the first charge to which he was appointed was the "Braes" or "rough Bounds" of Arisaig, where he remained but one year. He was removed in 1801 to Badenoch, where he remained till 1806. During this part of his missionary life he had no fixed place of abode, but went about amongst the Catholic families within his jurisdiction, attended by his boy or ghillie, who served at Mass and carried the vestments, etc., in a wallet on his back. From Badenoch he was sent in quality of professor to the seminary of Lismore, where Bishop John Chisholm then presided. In 1814 he succeeded Mr Philip Macrae, in the mission of Aigas, Strathglass, from which charge he was transferred to Braemar. In 1838, his increasing infirmities having rendered him unfit for active exertion, he was relieved from all missionary duty, and retired first to Ballogie, where he lived until 1847, when he went to live at Tombae, where he died on 9th September 1849.

Besides his labours as a clergyman, in which he distinguished himself by a zealous discharge of all his pastoral duties, Mr Maceachan has conferred great benefits, especially on the Highland portion of Scottish Catholics, by the numerous works which he published. Being an excellent Gaelic scholar, of which language he was an enthusiastic admirer, and being during his life particularly fond of study, he employed all the time he could spare from his other avocations, while on the mission, in translating into Gaelic several works of piety and of religious instruction. These translations are:

1. "The Abridgment of Christian Doctrine," which was printed while he was a missionary in Aigas.

2. "The Spiritual Combat," published in 1835.

3. "The Following of Christ," published in 1836.

4. A Prayer Book, which was prepared by him, but published by another priest.

5. "The Declaration of the British Catholic Bishops."

6. A small Gaelic Dictionary, printed in 1842. His more important Gaelic translations, still in MSS. at the time of his death, are the New Testament, and Challoner's "Meditations."

Such were the labours of this truly excellent man; of which the district of Arisaig, where he was born, has every reason to be proud.

The later priests of this district were: Rev. Angus Macdonald, 1877 to 1880; Rev Donald Mackay, 1880–

1882 ; Rev. Donald M'Pherson, 1882–1894 ; Rev. Angus Macdonald, 1894–1902 ; Very Rev. James Canon Chisholm, 1902–   .

To refer once again to the new church, the site was indeed most happily chosen. It adjoins the old pre-Reformation church of St Malrubber, which with its cemetery seems to form part of the new church grounds. The ancient church and cemetery being both of them full of antiquarian interest and of remains of Catholic ritual and observance, there is a peculiar propriety in the new and handsome church being placed alongside the old one. The two form an example of continuity which is very striking. Justly have the priests in more recent times loved to be buried at Arisaig ; there is probably no church in Great Britain which has such Catholic associations. It has ever been surrounded by an almost entirely Catholic population, which justly revered, in the time of Bishop Nicolson, as well as in the days previous to that, and in later times, the ruined church with its ancient tombs and cemetery. In 1700 they had been closed to Catholic ritual and services little more than one hundred years, whilst within the walls of the chapel certainly no other service than the Catholic had ever been held.

The church of Arisaig was entirely renovated in 1900, by Rev. Angus Macdonald, who inserted a most artistic stained-glass window in the East gable of the church, over the high altar, representing the Crucifixion, with Our Lady and St John on each side. The cost of this was borne by the Dowager Marchioness of Bute, who herself figures in it, kneeling on a *prie-Dieu* in an attitude of prayer.

It will not be out of place here to record the many benefits conferred on this mission by the Macdonald family, now of Glenaladale, but formerly residing at Borrodale, Arisaig, where they lived for several generations. Of this family were the brothers Archbishop Angus Macdonald and Bishop Hugh Macdonald, of whom further mention is made in the following chapter. It was whilst priest of Arisaig, where he built the present fine presbytery, that the former was called to be Bishop of Argyll, and he ever retained the greatest affection for the district. It is most dear also to the heart of every Highlander, being so closely associated with the history of the forty-five. It was at Borrodale, in the house of Bishop Macdonald's ancestors, that Prince Charlie held the first Council of War with the local chiefs, immediately before the Rising; it was at Arisaig, at the head of Loch nan Uamh, that he landed from Skye; it was from that same loch that he departed for France; and at Borrodale is the actual cave where he hid previous to his departure for France under the shelter of old Borrodale.

MOYDART

THE district of Moydart has been fully dealt with by Father Charles Macdonald, who for over forty years was priest in the district, and who was, most justly, respected and esteemed. The following letters of some of the earlier priests are, however, very interesting, and are given in full, as showing the close ties which existed between the priests educated at Propaganda, and the Cardinals who in turn presided over the College.

It will, however, be as well first to give a brief sketch of the history of the Catholic Faith in these districts, along with the succession of priests—which is now almost complete. The old chapel of St Finnan, which is the pre-Reformation Church of Moydart, still stands, a much-respected ruin in the beautiful island of Loch Shiel. Although the tradition is that the chapel has not been used for the past one hundred and fifty years—probably never since the Reformation—nevertheless the cemetery around it is still the chief place of burial for Catholics and Protestants alike, whilst within the ruined chapel are the old altar and the ancient bell, objects of veneration to all the inhabitants, irrespective of creed. Indeed the whole island, with its deep religious associations, forms a link through Reformation and pre-Reformation days to those of Saint Finnan himself, the patron and apostle of Moydart, and one of the first disciples of St Columba.

The first priests after the Reformation were those who did what they could, working indiscriminately all through

134

the Highlands—viz. Mr White, Mr Munro (or Rattray), Messrs Colgan, Conon and Kelly—all three from Ireland.[1] Mr Colin Campbell was priest in Moydart in 1728 ; Mr Neil MacPhee was there between 1731 and 1736, and Mr William Harrison visited the district in the years 1746 to 1750. In 1763 the Abbate Grant, in his Report to Propaganda, states that "the Catholics in these two districts [Arisaig and Moydart] number over 2,000. The priest who is there at present is Mr Alexander Macdonald, a man well learned and full of energy, who was educated at the Scots College, Rome." From this date onwards we have a regular succession of the priests who served this mission. Their names are inserted here, though fuller details are given in the following pages. Mr Austin Macdonald came in 1769 and remained till 1787. He was succeeded by Mr John Macdonald, who remained but four years and was succeeded by Mr Norman Macdonald, who for over forty years was priest of Moydart (1792–1834) and died there in 1834. During the last five years he was assisted by Mr Alexander Macdonald, who remained in charge till 1838, when he was succeeded by Mr Ranald Rankine (1838–1855). Mr Charles Macdonald had care of Moydart till 1892, and was succeeded by V. R. Provost Mackintosh, who at the time of writing is still in charge of this mission.

Of the above, Mr Austin Macdonald writes to the Cardinal Prefect of Propaganda in 1771 :

"EMINENT AND MOST REVEREND SIR,—Having last autumn written for the first time to your Eminence in

[1] Mr Devoyer was certainly in Moydart in 1689, and as he spent eighteen years in the Highlands he may have been all that time in this district.

fulfilment of my duty, I hope that my letter has long
since arrived. I now feel it my duty to write again in
fulfilment of the same obligation.

" As no change has taken place in my residence or in
my work it will be sufficient to repeat briefly what I said
in my last letter. As regards my health, so far, thanks
be to God, my native air suits me very well, and I have
not yet experienced the inconveniences which the change
of climate usually brings to our novices, at their first
coming back to this country from abroad. The place of
my residence is the centre of the country of Moydart, on
the West coast of Scotland, where according to my poor
abilities I act in quality of parish priest. It is, as I said
in my last letter a very mountainous district, twenty
miles long and four broad. Thank God, all the inhabitants are Catholics. There are 500 communicants,
without counting the children. We have Mass only on
Sundays and feasts, when we assemble in the most con-
venient places There, after an explanation of the
Gospel, Mass is said. The people go to Confession twice
in the year, at Easter and at Christmas. Within the
district a Minister resides usually, but there is no
danger from him, as regards my people, who hate him
from the bottom of their hearts. The greatest difficulty
of those beginning their priestly life here [as he was
doing] is the ignorance of the language, which, even
though it is our mother tongue, is not easily spoken by us
for some time, having left home as early as we did.

" As regards our Protestant neighbours, they are not
very bigoted; many are indeed well disposed towards
our Faith, and of these some are from time to time converted. Two things however are a great hindrance to

their conversion ; the first, the fear of their relations and of the Ministers, who appear, many of them, to be none too popular ; the other is the scarcity of the Missioners, for at the extreme East of this parish, all agree that if there was a resident priest, such as I cannot be, in a short time all the neighbouring district would return to the Catholic Faith, so that we may say with the Prophet, ' the harvest indeed is great, but the workmen are few, behold the country is now ready for the harvest.' This is all, your Eminence, that I need write at present. That the Lord God may preserve your Eminence is the constant prayer of your Eminence's devoted and humble servant,

AUSTIN MACDONALD.

" MOYDART, 10 *Sep.* 1771."

The obligation, referred to in the above letter, is that incumbent on all those educated at Propaganda, of writing once a year to the Superior of the College, to give an account of their work. It is due to this rule that we have several letters from those educated at the Urban College, as Propaganda was and still is called. Moreover these letters were always answered by the Cardinal Prefect, and thus a chain of correspondence grew up which is very striking. There is a tone of affectionate interest in many of the letters which makes them charming reading. Indeed the Catholics of Scotland, and of the whole British Empire, have little idea how much they owe to the College and Congregation of Propaganda. For two hundred and fifty years almost every matter of ecclesiastical interest concerning them was there decided, or at least confirmed. Thence came for years the only salary of their bishops and of their priests, and thence came the funds to support the little seminaries at Scalan, at Morar or Lismore, and to assist the Scots College in Rome. It was at Propaganda that many of the priests were educated, that the Bishops were nominated, and that their decisions were confirmed. The handsome square block of the Propaganda buildings, simple and unadorned as it is, may well be taken as a symbol of the solid lasting work which the Institution has achieved, not only in Scotland but in three-quarters of the Christian world. Over all the windows the crest of the founder, Pope Urban VIII.—the honey bee—may still be seen, a fitting device again to adorn an institution where so much quiet, unassuming work has been ceaselessly carried on. The present writer has frequently been delighted in reading the grateful thanks expressed to Propaganda by the bishops and priests of old, whilst he himself records with pleasure the care which has been taken in preserving the records of the past. In the archives of Propaganda may be seen to-day Reports and letters from the men who laboured so hard and under such great difficulties to save what little remained of Catholicism in Scotland, until there should come those happier days, which we have been spared to see. As one reads these Reports at the present time, and certainly there is a great charm in them, one cannot but feel the wish to make the labours and self-sacrifice of our predecessors in the mission of Scotland better known, and at the same time to awaken that gratitude towards Propaganda which they themselves were the first to acknowledge. The foregoing lines, which I jotted down at the time of my visit to the College, may fitly be inserted here when we are dealing with the letters of the first students educated within the College itself, and those of the Scots College, Rome.

The next letter of Austin Macdonald is dated Moydart, 10th August 1783.

"YOUR EMINENCE,—

"Having been educated at the Scots College, Rome, for about twelve years, it is now fourteen years since I returned to my native land of Moydart, where to the best of my abilities, I have laboured in the vineyard of the Lord. As far as I remember, I returned in the summer of the year 1769. This district, situated on the West Coast of the Highlands of Scotland, and of the Vicariate which takes its name from the Highlands, is bounded along its entire length by enemies of the Faith, having Catholics only on its Northern side. It extends about 24 miles from East to West and is some six miles broad. These miles being only approximate I cannot say more than that one of them suffices for a good hour's walk, it is very mountainous with a few valleys interspersed, royal roads there are as yet none. The only royal road is Loch Shiel, a fresh-water loch, 24 miles long, where when the weather is good, one can travel over a large part of the district. Thank God, we are all Catholics, except three or four strangers, and we number according to the list compiled this year, 1,450 souls, all most fervent in the Faith, of whom the greater number have been Catholics; and their parents before them, from time immemorial. They lead very innocent lives, and it is a great consolation to me to find them so ready to follow any advice I may give them.

" The language spoken here is the Highland or ancient Celtic, which, it is said, was formerly used on the borders of Italy. The upper classes generally speak English which is taught in the schools, and not the other, whence the people learn the elements of the faith with difficulty, and only viva voce. In vain have the Ministers several times tried to overcome this stronghold of the Faith by error, and for this end they established here an heretical Missionary with a good salary. On the other hand if they did not import strangers, he would have to shout to the rocks! Of the aforementioned number 250 of my people are interspersed among the heretics for a distance of at least thirty miles.

" On my arrival here I found this station without house, or church, without vestments, books or any of those things which help to forward the service of God. Indeed on account of the people being unaccustomed to subscribe, and on account of their poverty, it has cost me much labour and the greatest economy to rebuild this almost ruined church. Nevertheless by the help of God, and by patience and perseverance, I have been able to build three houses for the Congregation, one at each end and one in the centre, where the people assemble in turn. I have also built something of a house for myself, where however I cannot stay long at a time on account of the pressing calls from all sides; and on account of the devices employed by the heretics, especially when our people are dying. The Ministers do not take this in good part, and they have often tried to hinder me from entering their limits by threatening letters, but as the Mercy of God has preserved me so far, I have paid no heed to them in the past nor shall I do so in the future. The altar fittings

1. Old Gatehouse of Bishops home.

2. Front Screen built by Bishop, the Bridges etc. when it was private & his lordship was bringing then out

3. Bay added by the Macs.

4. Parts added by Lord MacLean

before the Bridleys built this house, in Summer they were in the Square.

SAMALAMAN LODGE

Showing former Seminary

To face page 141

which I have managed to get are less nice than I would wish, but necessity like a good theologian, solves every difficulty. During the past winter I secured the services of an old gentleman, as catechist ; he has done a great deal of good amongst the people. When I was able to administer the Sacraments twice a year, I did so, and when unable, I did so at least once. On two occasions I was forced through lack of priests to attend to neighbouring districts, but this year, thank God, I have myself been granted an assistant.

"Moreover to my great consolation the Vicar Apostolic of the Highland District has this year placed in my parish the Seminary, where he himself lives. This has already done great good and given an impulse to this corner of the Lord's vineyard, to the honour of God, and of His Church on earth, and will by His help give a still greater increase in the future.

" This is all of importance which I think I should now write to your Eminence, so begging God long to preserve you,

" I Remain your Eminence's humble servant,

"AUSTIN MACDONALD.

" MOYDART, 10 *August*, 1783."

An interesting letter of Bishop John MacDonald is extant regarding the chapel and priest's house at Moydart. It gives us a fair idea of the size of the buildings, if chapel and priest's house could be built for £60, even granted that the labour was free. The letter is as follows :—

" YOUR EMINENCE,

"I received from Daulensis [Bishop Hay] the very kind letter of Your Eminence in which you enquire by whose assistance Austin Macdonald built the chapel in his parish, as well as a house for himself. To this I have the pleasure of replying, that I am informed both by himself and by others, that his parishioners greatly assisted him in the work. They gave their services free in carrying the materials for the building, and subscribed about eight guineas amongst themselves. Otherwise he received nothing from any other source.

" From the time he came to the Mission he always desired to have a house of his own, and frequently told me so, in order to be more free to devote himself to his priestly duties, and to his own sanctification, which he has always had much at heart. To this end he stinted himself as much as possible and eventually saved up £30 sterling. This has all been spent on the building and I fear there may be some debt besides, which would easily happen in the case of a man, almost too anxious about religious matters, and at the same time little versed in business.

" He has already completed the chapel, but his own house is not yet finished , and I am told it will require another £30 to make it fit for habitation. Under these circumstances unless he obtains help from outside he will have to live in the greatest poverty. If your Eminence and the Sacred Congregation see fit to send him some pecuniary assistance, I can assure you that he greatly deserves it, and is really in sore need ; so that I feel he is well worthy of your generosity.

" JOHN, *Bishop of Tiberiop. Vicar. Apost.*

"SCALAN, 22 *July*, 1778."

The remark that he could not stay long at home on

account of the many calls from all sides seems to indicate that the people were rather loath to give up the earlier practice of having the priest to stay with them in their houses. We can well imagine that many a household which had for generations been accustomed to the visit of the priest for several days at a time would be slow to give up what they had probably come to consider their privilege. Hence even after he had a house of his own he would be invited to stay with his old friends, and probably found it necessary to lessen the frequency of these visits by degrees, rather than suddenly abandon them altogether.

The remark regarding there being no "royal road" in Moydart refers to the fact that at this period Government were making roads in many districts of the Highlands. It is scarcely realised at the present time that the first real road in the Highlands was that between Fort Augustus and Fort William, begun in 1725. Previous to that all intercourse was carried on by means of ponies; or by very rough tracks, so dangerous as to be little used.

The following extracts from letters of General Wade will illustrate this more clearly. Writing in 1726, he says: "I have inspected the new road between this place [Fort Augustus] and Fort William, and ordered it to be enlarged and carried on for four-wheel-carriages over the mountains on the South side of Loch Ness as far as the town of Inverness, so that before midsummer next, there will be a good coach road from that place, which before was not passable on horseback in many places."

A year later he writes: "The great road of communication is so far advanced; that I travelled to Fort William in my coach and six to the great wonder of the country people, who had never seen such a machine in these parts before. They ran from their houses close to the coach, and looking up, bowed with their bonnets to the coachman, little regarding us that were within. It is not unlikely that they looked upon him as a sort of Prime Minister that guided so important a machine." The whole system of making roads was of the greatest benefit to the Highland district. As Sir Kenneth Mackenzie has justly remarked : " He [Wade] was the originator of a system which received immense development after his death, and with which his name remained connected in the public memory; long after he had ceased to share in directing its operations. The benefits he conferred on this part of the country in opening it up by means of roads, and thus bringing it into line with the rest of the kingdom, can hardly be overestimated. No other action ever taken by the Government has done so much for the material welfare of the Highlands." True as this undoubtedly is, we should not overlook the fact that it was the absence of roads and the consequent inaccessibility of the various districts, that helped more than any other cause to keep these districts free from persecution, and to secure to the Catholics in them the almost undisturbed exercise of their religion.

The next letter of Mr Austin Macdonald is dated April, 1787.

" YOUR EMINENCE,

" Having at last a little breathing time between my many duties, it is full time that I remembered my obligation of giving an account to you of what I am doing.

I am very late in doing so, it is true, but this is due rather to the number of calls upon my time, than to any want of will on my part.

"On account of the emigration last summer of the people of Knoydart to Canada, along with their priest, it fell to me in the autumn to attend to those who were left behind, and during the winter to the people of Moydart as well. Although not less than 600 Catholics went to America, still I administered the Sacraments to over 500 souls who remained. The overpopulation of these districts, together with the oppression of the landlords are the principal causes of the departure of so many, not only among the Catholics, but also among the Protestants. I have some idea that it will be best for me to change my residence this Whitsuntide, and to betake myself to Knoydart, although I have now resided in Moydart just eighteen years. If I should actually go, I shall inform your Eminence in due course. Praying God meantime for your welfare, I remain your Eminence's most humble and devoted servant,

"AUSTIN MACDONALD.

"MOYDART, 6th April, 1787."

A year later he wrote again :

" YOUR EMINENCE,

"The reply which you deigned to send to my last letter, and the approval therein contained of my work, such as it is, brought me no little consolation, and added a fresh incentive to my former ones, always to work to the best of my power for the increase of God's glory and the advancement of Holy Church. Moreover it will

K

make the duty of reporting my work all the easier. For 17 years I shall have laboured in the district of Moydart, but for the past two years, with the consent of my Superiors, I have removed to that of Knoydart. Here formerly Mr Alexander Macdonald was stationed, a pupil of the Scots College, Rome, but he has gone to America with 604 of his parishioners.

" I find that there are still in that district about 500 communicants, not counting children. They are Catholics of good and simple lives and most steadfast in the Faith. Six miles distant from them is the mission of Kintail, where only twenty years ago there was but one Catholic At present there are from 300 to 400 converts, steadfast also in the Faith, although they are as yet but imperfectly instructed. It has fallen to me to take care of this Mission also, and that to my great satisfaction, since there cannot as yet be a resident priest. In these two places I shall continue to work, and if anything should happen, I shall mention it on a future occasion. Your Eminence's humble servant,

" AUSTIN MACDONALD."

It is strange that of the letters of priests still extant in Propaganda the greater number should be of two Moydart men. The second successor of Mr Austin Macdonald was Mr Norman Macdonald, of whom the following three letters speak of his life and work among the Catholics of Moydart :

" MOST EMINENT AND MOST REVEREND SIR,

" Some months ago I received the letter with which your Eminence deigned to favour me, bearing date 8th Dec. 1804. From this I understand that your Eminence does not consider the poverty of a Missioner as a valid reason to excuse him from writing to Rome every year, according to the obligation which he has contracted, and to this decision I acquiesce as to the will of God. In giving some account of my state I have little more to say than what I wrote in my last letter to the late Cardinal Borgia, whose death at Lyons I read of in the paper to my great regret. The mission at present entrusted to my care lies along the coast of the Atlantic and is about 30 miles round. The number of Catholics dispersed here and there in this mission is about 800, amongst whom there are some converts. Recently I visited a large island where all are Protestants, with the exception of about 30 Catholics, amongst whom I had the great pleasure of receiving to the Sacraments a lady recently converted to the Faith, who had married a Catholic. What surprises the Protestants is that the lady is the daughter of one of their Ministers, who was not able to stop her conversion. Yet the father greatly loved her, and she is not without hopes of seeing her father also converted one day.

" I greatly hope that the example of this lady will induce others to follow her in the way of Truth. The distances are so great, and the country I have to traverse so rough, whilst there is not a single road, that I am nearly worn out, and my health has become very uncertain. Only the remembrance of the reward ' exceeding great ' which I look for, is able to sustain me amid such labours. If the Congregation has any alms to distribute, I trust they will remember the first Scotsman who had the honour of being educated at the venerable college of Propaganda.

" Your Eminence's humble servant

" Norman Macdonald."

The obligation of writing to Rome applied seemingly not only to the Alumni of Propaganda itself but also to those educated at the Scots College in that city, as is seen from the letter of Austin Macdonald which precedes this one, and from other letters also, especially one, of Alexander Macdonald, priest in Arisaig.

Mr Norman Macdonald's next letter is dated 28th Nov. 1817. After the usual compliments, he says : " At all events I can assure you that from the time of the so-called Reformation in this kingdom, our holy religion has never enjoyed so great peace and liberty as it has enjoyed for some time past. Indeed, as the Protestants abandon the idea of the first reformers, they become broader-minded and more liberal towards all sorts of religions, inasmuch as in the capital, where in 1779 all was fire and sword against the Catholics, these have just erected with the approval of the Protestants themselves and with the help of some of them, nice large churches with organs, where occasionally Protestants come to hear the preaching, the reading of Scripture and of holy doctrine. We cannot indeed sufficiently thank the Lord for having done us so great a favour. As regards my present occupation, I have charge of the same parish, which I have now had for over 25 years. It is very extensive, but the number of Catholics who are dispersed, here and there, is not proportionate to its size, being, according to the reckoning which I made last year, only 950, of whom 34 are converts. Of these latter, I hope for an increase shortly.

" We preach here in the Celtic language, which is very expressive, and is our native tongue, as it was of our famous poet, Ossian. I find indeed that much of the Latin language is derived from it, both having many roots in common.

" Your Eminence's humble servant,

" NORMAN MACDONALD."

I have transcribed the Reverend Gentleman's remarks on the connection between Gaelic and Latin as he set them down. His reference to Ossian is interesting, as the controversy regarding his works was at its height during this period.

The next letter, the last which I found of this faithful " first Scots Alumnus of Propaganda," as he so regularly styles himself, was written four years after the preceding. There is something very charming in the care of Propaganda for the old priest, as the subsidy to which he refers was evidently a special grant to himself, the usual yearly allowance being always sent through the Vicars Apostolic, and distributed by them. On another occasion we find Propaganda contributing to the building of a church for one of its own Alumni, whilst as each Vicar Apostolic was appointed a grant was made to provide him with pontificals. Certainly this was done in the case of Bishop Hugh McDonald. whose letter thanking Propaganda for the gift is still preserved.

" YOUR EMINENCE,

" With the greatest pleasure I received the much esteemed letter of your Eminence, dated 20th May last, for which I am especially grateful in view of the satisfaction which you deigned to express as to my poor endeavours in this mission. Shortly afterwards I received proof of your sincere kindness and sympathy in the very opportune subsidy which you graciously accorded me. May Our Good God fully reward your Eminence in Heaven for having sent such subsidy ; I shall indeed ever be grateful for it and also for so many other undeserved benefits.

" As regards the state of my health, I was fairly well during the summer and autumn, but since the beginning of winter I have been much troubled with rheumatism, and toothache, caused by the successive rain, frost and snow, which continue almost uninterruptedly in these parts except during the summer. I would have written much sooner to the Sacred Congregation but I was waiting time after time, that the Bishop, according to his promise, would come in the autumn to administer Confirmation, and I might be able to give the number of those confirmed. I have thus been forced to wait till now, since the Bishop did not come until Advent ; immediately after that I had to go and give Holy Communion during Christmastide in various places of this extensive parish. These hindrances together with the poor state of my health made me put off writing until now. As regards the number of those confirmed, there were 67 men and 77 women, their ages ranging from 8 to 70, amongst them being some Converts the sight of whom made the Protestants 'grind their teeth.' There are still some others to be confirmed, but they are dispersed, here and there, at such distances that they could not come and return in a short winter's day. The number of souls committed to my care is about 960 ;

I say about, because I hope shortly to add other Converts to fill up the number. 'The harvest is indeed great, but the labourers are few' and I am extremely sorry that Propaganda is not in a position to receive at least one youth from this Vicariate.

"I have nothing further to add except that I fear the weight of years and my weak health, which causes a great trembling in my hands, will prevent me from writing to the Sacred Congregation in future. But whatever happens please be assured that I am resigned to the Will of God.

" Your Eminence's humble servant .

"NORMAN MACDONALD.

"*First Scots Alumnus of Propag.*

"MOYDART, 5th Jan. 1821."

This letter is endorsed: "Answered 7th April, 1821."

But to return to our regular succession of priests, Mr Austin Macdonald emigrated to America shortly after the date of the last of his letters given above—he was succeeded by Mr John Macdonald, who, according to his obituary notice in 1835, had spent five years in Moydart. Mr Norman Macdonald was there no less a period than thirty-eight years (1792-1829). Being disabled by age and infirmities—he had previously served for five years in Uist and Arisaig—he resigned in 1829, and died in 1834, being buried in the chapel of Dorlin, near Castle Tirrim.

Mr Alexander Macdonald was priest in Moydart from 1829 to 1838. He was a native of Lochaber, and after studying a few years at Lismore, he went, in November, 1816, to the Scots College, Valladolid, where he remained till 1822. In 1824 he was ordained by Bishop Ranald

Macdonald. He spent a few years teaching at Lismore, and as Assistant in Arisaig, and came to Moydart, as stated above, in 1829. In 1838 he was succeeded by Mr Ranald Rankine, who in his turn emigrated to Australia, in 1855. Father Charles Macdonald was priest in Moydart from 1860 to 1892, when he was succeeded by the present priest, the venerable and justly respected Provost Mackintosh, who at the date of writing has the wonderful record of fifty-four years spent in the most laborious districts of the Highlands.

Of the colleges at Samalaman and Lismore a short account may fittingly be inserted here.

Bishop Alexander Macdonald settled at Samalaman in 1783. In 1786 he writes to Mr Thomson, the agent in Rome, that he had then five or six boys, which were as many as his " narrow income " allowed him to keep. In 1789 he began to enlarge the house, and wrote in the July of that year: " Since ever I was made Bishop, I always lamented the distress of the Highland District for want of anything of a decent house wherein some of the clergy and I could convene from time to time in order to deliberate about matters regarding the good of religion in these parts ; but the low state of my finances prevented my attempting anything of this kind till the beginning of June last, when I began to build on this small farm. By this time the wall is near finished and in a month hence I believe it will be slated. It is allowed to be very handsome of its size ; its dimensions are length about 35 feet ; breadth 16 feet ; height of the side walls 18 feet. I shall endeavour, God willing, to finish the shell of it without loss of time."

The furnishings for the new house were bought in

SAMALAMAN COLLEGE

Glasgow in October, 1790—the Bishop tells his colleague Bishop Geddes in a letter of that date—and were sent to Greenock and put on board a sloop belonging to Mr Andrew Macdonald to be brought by sea to Samalaman. But the good Bishop was not to have the pleasure of even settling in his new house, for I am assured locally that he had not moved from the old house into the new, when death overtook him in 1791.

Bishop John Chisholm after his consecration took up his residence at Samalaman, but in 1794 he complains of the miserable state of the seminary, due, no doubt, to the death of Bishop Macdonald, while it was still incomplete. In 1798 Bishop Chisholm was already looking for another site. At this period Mr Angus Macdonald, who had been in charge of the seminary since it was reopened at Samalaman, was taken ill, and the Bishop writes that he has been obliged to " allow him to roam about a little." Several letters of Angus Macdonald exist, describing his life at Samalaman, which I hope to publish at a later date.

After the college had been transferred, in 1803, to Lismore, Samalaman was let by Clanranald to a Mr Chisholm, and he was succeeded by Mr M'Quarry, of Mull. Mr Stewart then bought the property, and went to live there. In his time the building was struck by lightning and great damage done. The rooms on either side of Mr Stewart's bedroom were wrecked, but his own room was absolutely untouched. He believed that a special blessing was on that room, as it was the one occupied by the bishops in the college days. He was unmarried, and left the estate to his nephew, Mr M'Lean, from whose family it was purchased by Lord M'Laren.

Amongst those who studied at Samalaman, we find the names of the Rev. John Lamont, who died in Glengarry in 1820 ; Rev. Anthony Macdonald, for over thirty years priest of Eigg and Canna ; Rev. Angus MacEachan or Macdonald, who afterwards became a bishop in Canada ; Rev. Charles Macdonald, a native of the district, who spent most of his life in Knoydart. Rev. John MacEachan or Macdonald was educated first at Buorblach, and afterwards at the Scots College, Valladolid. He was for seven years Professor of Moral Philosophy there, and on his return was appointed to the same position in Samalaman. In the " Liber Defunctorum " it is recorded that the Rev. Donald Macdonald died at Samalaman on 22nd January 1785. The Rev. Allan Macdonald died there on 22nd March 1788 ; Right Rev. Alexander Macdonald, Bishop of Polemo and Vicar Apostolic of the Highland District, departed this life there on 12th September 1791.

In addition to the College Chapel there was also a small thatched building which served as a church for the congregation. In the illustration the original buildings are those on the left ; the two portions with higher roofs were added, the one on the left by Mr M'Lean, the other by the late Lord M'Laren.

Regarding the transfer of the seminary from Samalaman to Lismore, this took place in 1803. The island of Lismore is situated nearly opposite the town of Oban, whence the passenger steamers sail for the Outer Hebrides. It certainly had that advantage. The site included a substantial house, built a few years before by the proprietor, Campbell of Dunstaffnage, an excellent garden, and, according to Angus Macdonald, " a few acres of good ground." He also states that the island had been the residence of the pre-Reformation Bishops of Argyll, and that its name, Lismore, meant "a large garden." It is certainly a most picturesque situation. His letter is written: "Lismorea, ex Collegio Killechiarensi." The price paid for the house and ground was £5,000, which was considered very reasonable.

Lismore continued to be the residence of the Highland Vicar Apostolic and his seminary until the transfer to Blairs in 1829. The house is still standing, and is used as a farmhouse. The old chapel is the present dining-room ; close by the two Bishops Chisholm are buried.[1] As a college, Lismore sent some of the best priests to the Highland Mission, as the following list will show :—

JOHN CHISHOLM, who for fifty years was priest in South Uist, entered Lismore in 1805, and was there ordained by Bishop John Chisholm in 1814. He continued there as master until 1817.

DONALD FORBES, for over fifty years priest of Lochaber, was educated at Lismore, where he entered in 1806 and was ordained in 1816.

JAMES M‘GREGOR, who had the charge of the northern portion of South Uist for forty years, entered Lismore in 1808, and was there ordained by Bishop Æneas Chisholm in 1816. He continued as master there till 1819.

NEIL MACDONALD, who died in 1863, entered Lismore in 1812 and remained there till 1816, when he went to Valladolid.

---

[1] The burial ground containing the remains of the two bishops and others is a small, walled-in plot immediately behind the house. It measures twenty-four feet square The walls were repaired and the whole neatly gravelled at the cost of the present Bishop of Argyle and the Isles, R.R. George Smith.

DONALD MACKAY, born at Frobost, in South Uist, 1804. Entered Lismore, 1823, and proceeded to Propaganda, where he had a most distinguished course.

JOHN FORBES was ordained at Lismore in 1815.

RANALD RANKINE studied at Lismore, and was later sent to Valladolid.

DONALD MACDONALD entered Lismore in 1816, and later completed his studies in Rome.

WILLIAM MACKINTOSH, for forty years priest of Arisaig, spent the years 1821 to 1826 as a student at Lismore.

ALEXANDER GILLIES, priest of Eigg from 1842 to 1881, entered Lismore in 1825, and went from there to Rome.

ANGUS MACKENZIE and ARCHIBALD CHISHOLM began their student life at Lismore, and were thence transferred to Blairs. The former had entered in 1826.

BISHOP WILLIAM FRASER had charge of the studies at Lismore for several years previous to 1820, when he emigrated to Cape Breton.

In 1855 there were two chapels in Moydart, the Castle Chapel, near the ruins of Castle Tirrim, and the Langal Chapel, which still exists and is now used as an alms-house. There was at this period a station at Glenuig, close to the former seminary of Samalaman. Here, in 1862, a new chapel was built, of which the neighbouring scenery undoubtedly formed the greatest beauty. "It commands a magnificent view over Glenuig Bay," so runs the account of its opening in 1862, "which separates Arisaig from Moydart, whilst the waters of the Loch reach to within a few feet of the chapel."

The year following, the present very pretty church was opened in the parent mission. "The district of Moydart," so runs the Directory account, "in the extreme S.W.

LISMORE COLLEGE AND CHAPEL

Now part of Kilcheran Lodge

To face page 156

portion of Invernessshire, is full of interest, not only from its romantic scenery, and from its having been the country of the adventures of the unfortunate Charles Stuart, during his flight after the Battle of Culloden, but still more to the Catholics, as one of the few places where the people have throughout all the dark times of poverty and persecution, clung to the Old Faith.

" This fact is the more remarkable because part of the district, where the new church is built, and which is wholly Catholic, is only separated from the entirely Protestant districts of the south, by the narrow loch and river Shiel.

" The Catholics of Moydart, who have been compelled to assemble for Mass since they have been able to do so at all, in small and inconvenient buildings, hardly deserving the name of chapels, thrown up at random here and there in different districts, have now a handsome parish church. It is well suited to all their wants, and forms with the presbytery and schools attached, a complete parochial establishment, such as certainly does not exist elsewhere in the Western Highlands amongst Catholics, Episcopalians or Presbyterians. The church and priest's house, as well as the school buildings, have been built at the sole expense of the present proprietor of the estate of Loch Shiel, J. R. Hope Scott, Esq.

" The wish expressed by Mr Austin Macdonald in 1771, that a church should be built at the extreme east of his district, was eventually carried out in 1874, when the present beautiful church was opened at Glenfinnan. It was built at the sole expense of Rev. D Macdonald, brother of the laird of Glenaladale, and is a really striking building, whilst the site is all that could be desired for picturesque beauty. The church is situated on an elevated platform, overhanging the upper end of Loch Shiel, in the midst of some of the most charming and romantic scenery in Scotland."

With pardonable pride, the Directory of 1874 continues : " The pipes used on the morning of the opening of the Church were the identical pipes played at the first gathering of the Clans on this same spot in 1745. They were played again on the fatal field of Culloden, and were ever afterwards carefully preserved as a most precious heirloom in the family of Glenaladale. By a singular and unpremeditated coincidence, the gathering for the opening of the Church took place on the anniversary of the eventful gathering of the Clans in the Stuart Cause."

Another incident of note at this opening was the presence of the two nephews of the founder, Angus and Hugh Macdonald, both of them later bishops, and men of endless energy in the cause of religion. The Right Rev. Angus Macdonald as Bishop of Argyle and the Isles had within his See all the districts with which we are now dealing, and in almost every one of them he left the impress of his character. New churches arose under his influence, new missions were opened, and a spirit of fervour was enkindled in priests and people alike, which was very remarkable. Endless were the journeyings by sea and by land which the Bishop performed in the visitation of his flock. From mainland to island, from town to hamlet he went, serving his people, preaching to them and confirming them, in winter as in summer, in fair weather as in foul. A man of greater physical strength might easily have felt in fewer years the strain of such manifold activities.

His transference to the archdiocese of St Andrews and Edinburgh was little less than a calamity for the former Highland district, whilst his death in Edinburgh only eight years later, at the early age of fifty-six, was a grievous loss to the Catholics of Scotland. His brother, Bishop Hugh Macdonald, of Aberdeen, was fully his equal in apostolic zeal and fervent piety, and his death in 1898 was most deeply regretted. I have noted elsewhere ("Ancient Catholic Homes of Scotland") what a wonderful record for religious vocations this family possesses. From the time when the young laird, Angus, became a priest about 1675 (*see* p. 174) there has seldom been a generation which did not give a priest to the Church in Scotland; whilst of the children and grand-children of John, Laird of Glenaladale, who died in 1830, three were nuns, and six were priests, of whom three became bishops. One can but hope that Providence will raise up from amongst the Catholic Highlands many a priest and many a bishop to follow in the lines of these fine characters; men of whom the Catholics of Scotland have just reason to be proud.

GLENGARRY

GLENGARRY, like all the other Catholic districts of the Highlands of Scotland, owed a great deal to Father Francis White, of whom it is fitting that a fuller record be inserted here. The epitome of his life is thus given in Gordon's "Catholic Church in Scotland," under date 1654. "Mr White, an Irish Lazarian, was brought from Spain, together with Mr Dermit Gray, by the Lord M'Donald this year; he converted many to the Faith and confirmed others in it. He disappeared in 1657, appeared again in 1662, disappeared again in 1664, appeared again in 1668, and continued in the Highland Mission till he died, on January 28th, 1679. He was held in great veneration in the Highlands, and his picture was kept in a room of the Castle of Glengarry, called 'Mr White's Room,' until that castle was burned in 1745."

These words I had often read, and had as often wondered if more would ever be known of this individual whose biographical notice seemed so mysterious. It was accordingly with great pleasure that I found among the archives of Propaganda many papers relating to him and his companion, who would seem frequently to have passed by the name of Grey, though his real name was Dugan. Lately I have learned that letters of these two fathers occur in the French life of St Vincent of Paul, by Abelly, and that these have been presented to the

English-speaking public by Rev. Patrick Boyle, C.M., in his work, "St Vincent and the Vincentians." It would thus appear that there exists material sufficient for a far more complete life of one who rendered signal service to the Catholics in the Highlands and Islands of Scotland.

In 1650 St Vincent of Paul wrote to the Congregation of Propaganda that in compliance with their request for missionaries, he had selected two religious, Father Francis White and Father Dermit Dugan, and he begged that the necessary faculties be granted to them. In 1652 Father Dugan wrote to St Vincent: "I have already in my former letters informed your Reverence of the happy issue of our journey from Paris here; but since I fear that these may not have reached you, and especially the last one, I shall tell you again in a few words how after having remained a long time in Holland, awaiting an opportunity of embarking, at last we were enabled to set out and we arrived here happily. This was due to the favour of the Chieftain recently converted, called the Chief of Glengarry, who took us under his protection, and who showed us such great kindness that words fail to express it. . . .

"God has already deigned to employ us for the conversion of the father of the Laird of Glengarry. He was an old man of 90, brought up from childhood in heresy, but very charitable to the poor. We instructed him and reconciled him to the Church. His weakness, which was already very great, soon after carried him to the grave, after he had been fortified by all the Sacraments of the Church and had given great proofs of his sorrow for having lived so long in heresy, and of the great joy which he felt at dying a Catholic. . . .

L

"Shortly after this I was overtaken by an illness, which quickly reduced me to the last extremity, without my being able to see a doctor, because there are none in these Highland districts for 90 miles round, nor are there any in the Hebrides. But if a few were found in Paris who were willing to come here, besides the great utility of their labours for the body, they would also be able to assist in the conversion of souls.

"Having by God's help somewhat recovered, I left my companion Mr Francis White in the Highlands of Scotland, whilst I went, conformably to my orders, to the Hebrides. . . ."

This and other letters describe the great work accomplished by Father White, who, however, in 1655—at the beginning of Lent—was seized at Gordon Castle, and led prisoner to Aberdeen, and thence to Edinburgh How long he remained in prison is not known, but the letters of the time point to the fact of his being set at liberty soon after. But if, as there is reason to suppose, he had gone to Gordon Castle to meet a priest and make his own Easter Confession, the circumstance of his arrest must have appeared additionally hard. We find him later complaining, as one of his greatest hardships, that it was with difficulty that he could see a priest once a year for the good of his own soul. His arrest on this occasion must have impressed him with the fact that, whatever sufferings his field of labour might entail, and they were many, he was in the Outer Isles, at least fairly safe from arrest.

At a somewhat later date (1665), we have numerous letters of Father White and of his schoolmaster in Glengarry. The former writes: "I give infinite thanks to your Reverence not only for having procured me an allowance, but also for having established the school-master, whom I have placed in that situation where I think to make my own residence for the most part. In truth you would rejoice greatly to see these poor children; how they advance in piety and learning, how quick they are at answering with texts from Scripture and of the Fathers all questions about our Holy Faith, and that by the help of a catechism which I have written for them, and which they commit to memory. . . .

"I beg your Reverence to excuse Ewen M'Alaister, the schoolmaster, for not having written before now the names of his scholars, and of their parents, but he fears to commit these matters to paper, lest the letters be inter-cepted. . . . Your Reverence should strive to have some youths educated in the houses recently established in Paris, especially in St Lazarre. It would indeed be a well-founded reason to appeal to the authority of the Holy See, to make them come out and work here, to succour these good people in their extreme spiritual necessity, well disposed as they are to the Holy Faith. If I had fifteen I could employ them with profit, and to the advancement of religion, and all would have more to do than they could manage. Indeed I protest, for the discharge of my conscience, that if I had help I could in a short time with the grace of God, bring back to the bosom of Holy Church, the people of all these Highlands and Islands. I see myself daily called to places to which I have to refuse to go, as indeed I could not visit them once in two years, and satisfy those who are there converted."

Father White had, as stated above, decided to make

his headquarters at Glengarry. Now to anyone who knows this part of the West Highlands it would seem incredible that any priest should attempt to serve the immense district which had fallen to the care of the worthy Vincentian from a point in itself so inaccessible, and no doubt it was only sheer necessity that made Father White think of doing so. At Invergarry, however, he was under the powerful protection of the laird of Glengarry, recently created Lord Macdonell and Aros, a nobleman of undoubtedly great power and of still greater pretensions, to whom the rôle of Protector of the Catholics in the Highlands would have been quite congenial. In any case Father White settled there with his schoolmaster, and a pleasant picture is presented of these two working together in the interests of the Catholic Church at a time when such co-operation was so sorely needed and yet so scarce. Where else, indeed, in Great Britain, could there be found, at this period, a Catholic school, with a Catholic schoolmaster, presided over by a Catholic priest?

Two letters of the worthy schoolmaster are extant. In one, dated 14th June 1665, he says: " I have received your Reverence's letter, and from my heart I thank you not only for the care and trouble which you have taken to procure me a salary and to keep me in this place, but also for the good and fatherly advice you give me in your most kind letter. . . . The place where I am teaching is the house of the Lord Macdonell, called Invergarry, in the district of Glengarry in the County of Inverness, thirty miles distant from the city of that name. The number of my scholars is small at present, being only twenty-four, but I hope that the number will be greater when his lordship returns from the Court in England. The scholars are of the names of Macdonald, Cameron, Macmartin, Fraser, Scott, Stuart, and Maciver. . . . Having no other books with which to teach the children to read, I have been obliged to teach two boys from an heretical catechism, a book much in use in the islands, as also from a Psalter in rhyme, and the book of Proverbs translated by the heretics into English, but with the precaution that I do not allow them to learn anything from these books by heart.

" Mr White is writing some very good questions in the manner of a catechism, for the instruction of the boys on Sundays and Feast days. Some of the boys are learning Grammar and the rudiments of Latin, with suitable authors ; others only learn to read and write. As their mother tongue is Gaelic, it is most difficult to teach them, with that as a foundation, the Scotch and English languages. But once they have learned these they are very easy to teach and very tractable. Above all they take great pleasure in learning the Catholic Faith and doctrine. Thus they learn with ardour and great enthusiasm the above-mentioned Catechism of Controversy."

Many thoughts are suggested by this first Report of a Catholic schoolmaster in the Highlands. Catholic Catechisms were long difficult to obtain in Scotland. More than one hundred years were to elapse before the question of printing one was raised. The difficulty of teaching Gaelic-speaking children in English still continues, and is all the more accentuated when, as not unfrequently happens, the teacher does not know any Gaelic "as a foundation." Bishop Hugh Macdonald, of Morar, who had himself gone through the process, frequently wrote in the following century, begging the authorities in Rome to be considerate to the boys whom he sent out to be priests ; for, inasmuch as they only knew Gaelic, with some smattering of English, they were at a great disadvantage.

How long M‘Alaister continued his school it is not easy to say, for these were troublous times in the Highlands, especially in Glengarry, where English soldiers were almost continually quartered on account of the laird's well-known Jacobite sympathies. Father White continued at his post till his excessive labours brought him, prematurely, it would seem, to the grave. The Prefect of the Mission writes of him, in 1676 : " Then there is Francis White, who for over twenty years has gathered, and still gathers, a most abundant harvest of souls in the West Highlands ; a truly Apostolic man, although broken down by hard work, his strength reduced by age and ill-health, greatly esteemed by all, even by the heretics, and much revered by them." Three years later the same writer announced the death of the worthy priest in the following terms : " The good Mr Francis White died towards the end of last January. After the event I went in fearful weather to visit the localities which he used to frequent in order to console as best I could the poor people he served for so many years. God's peace be with him. If any of his countrymen could be sent to take his place, it would be a great help to us. Others, as you are aware, are of no use to us, as they do not know the language."

The next account which we have of the Mission of Glengarry, and also the most detailed, is contained in the very interesting Report on the Highland Mission made

by Mr Alexander Leslie in 1677. He had come to the
Mission about 1670, and was thus a very young man to
be entrusted with so important a duty. Yet his Report
shows great determination and a charming gaiety of
disposition, which enabled him to overcome all difficulties.
He later went to Rome, whence he returned in August,
1681. In 1689 he was thrown into prison, and was not
liberated till 1691. In the register of priests he is
entered as Alex. Leslie, "Hardboots." He served in
succession the Missions of Enzie, Strathbogie, Banff,
and, dying in 1702, on 14th April, he was buried in
Enzie. He had been forty years on the Scotch Mission.

After stating his surprise at being appointed visitor,
and giving details of certain preparatory arrangements,
he continues : " I stayed in Banffshire until the middle
of Lent 1678 and then started for Inverness, through
the country of Moray. From Inverness I wrote to Mr
Robert Munro, a Highland Missionary, asking him to
meet me at the Bog of Gight in the Enzie, some time in
April. This he did, and I must confess that I could not
have visited the Highlands without him.

"Whilst I was in Inverness, I ministered to many
Catholics, who had not seen a priest for a long time.
This was especially the case with one gentleman and his
wife who had come a distance of 40 Scotch miles—about
80 Italian miles—to see if perchance they might find a
priest in Inverness, not having seen one for over two
years. They came across me quite accidentally, and
were so filled with joy that they could not restrain their
tears. It was indeed with difficulty that I could restrain
my own emotion, all the more when I thought of the rest
of these poor Catholics, so neglected that one might say

they were entirely abandoned. This consideration forced me to remain in Inverness longer than I had intended. My stay was however a great consolation to those most excellent and devout Catholics, who flocked in from all the surrounding country, making their Confessions, receiving Holy Communion, hearing Mass and giving themselves up entirely to devotions and prayers. Such was their fervour—indeed such was the fervour of all the Catholics in the Highlands—that it was difficult to say Mass without distraction. Their sighs and their ejaculations interrupted the Celebrant to such an extent, that it was often necessary to speak sharply to them, and to check them, if one would finish the Holy Sacrifice.

" Leaving Inverness, I betook myself to the Bog of Gight, the property of the Marquis of Huntly. This castle is on the banks of the River Spey, which is here the boundary of the county of Moray. On my arrival I found Mr Munro, the Highland Missionary, and for the space of eight days we rested discussing the work before us. We then started direct through Moray to Inverness, where we had to lay hid for some days, whilst we made provision for our journey into the Highlands. In particular we had to provide ourselves with clothes after the fashion of these people. They dress quite differently from the Lowlanders, and more in the style of the ancient Romans, as far as one can judge from the statues of the latter. We all had to dress in this style, even our servants and guides.

" When our preparations were completed, we set out along the bank of the River Ness until we came to the shores of the lake from which that river flows, and here we fell in with Mr Francis White, with whom he had a long consultation, and arranged some further details regarding our journey through the Highlands and Islands.

"From here we sent on our horses by a longer road, whilst, in order to shorten the journey, we ascended a mountain so steep that often we had to climb on hands and knees. We now entered the district called the Aird, fourteen long and weary miles from Inverness. We were received at the house of Sir Alexander Fraser, of Kinnaries, and treated with great kindness. Sir Alexander had once visited Rome and had there made the acquaintance of my brother, and on this account was highly pleased to meet me.

[*Note.*—Mr William Mackay writes as follows : "Colonel Fraser of Kinnaries—or Kinerras, as the name now appears on the Valuation Roll—was proprietor of that estate in 1678. Kinerras is in the parish of Kiltarlity, and has for generations formed part of the Lovat estates. Fraser also owned Kinmylies, near Inverness, which he sold to David Polson in 1688. He was also proprietor of Abriachan, which he sold to the Laird of Grant. He was alive in 1699. I did not know that he was entitled to be called Sir Alexander Fraser. He does not appear as such in the Valuation Roll of the County of Inverness of the year 1691, or in any other references which I have come across."]

"Two days afterwards we passed through mountainous tracks into the district of Strathglass. The Chief here is a most zealous Catholic, and so are practically all his vassals, having been reconciled to the Church by the missionary, Munro. I stayed here eight or ten days to obtain full information, and what I learned was most satisfactory. At this stage of our journey we had to leave our horses behind, as our road for the future was over precipitous mountains, and almost impenetrable forests. Further we here put off our Lowland dress and donned the Highland costume.

"From Strathglass we continued our journey in the direction of Invergarry. The weather was very adverse, the wind blowing a hurricane and the snow falling in blinding showers—this too when we were well on in May. We found that we could not reach Invergarry in one day, so we stopped at Pitmains, some miles short of our destination. Next day we arrived at Invergarry, and there I intended to stay five days in order to receive many reports from the Chief, a most zealous Catholic, of tried prudence, faith and constancy. I fell ill however and remained very feeble with a continuous fever for fourteen days. Though I then began to feel better, yet I was so weak that I could scarcely stand on my feet, much less travel in a country, where it is all ascending or descending precipitous mountains.

"Lady Macdonel, a most pious Catholic, tried to persuade me to go back, saying that I should be a dead man before I reached the Islands. Indeed many of the Catholics had prophesied the same before I reached Inverness. But Lord Macdonel encouraged me, and persuaded me not to give in, saying that in six days I should regain not only my health, but my strength as well. He then reprimanded those who were persuading me to the contrary, and especially her Ladyship, telling them that it was far better for me and for them, if 1 did die on the way, rather than turn back. If I went back, Rome would conclude that the country was the inaccessible haunt of rude savages, and would send no priests to them at all. He had no difficulty in persuading me to follow his advice, as I had already made up my mind rather to risk a hundred lives than fail in my duty to the Holy See. Over and above the motive of obedience there was the compassion I felt for these poor people. Every day something new came to my knowledge, their great need of priests, and how well they had deserved that Rome should send them some, their great piety and their insatiable thirst for the Holy Sacraments and for religious instruction. All this redoubled my courage, and filled me with constancy in the prosecution of my mission. My weakness however was so great that for the first week, our day's journey was but short; indeed the first stage from Invergarry was only five miles. By the grace of God my health improved as Lord Macdonel had foretold, and as it improved our stages also lengthened."

So much for the Report of Mr Alexander Leslie, which I have had occasion to quote regarding other districts visited by him. With reference to the school in Glengarry some very interesting letters exist, proving the strange fact that as early as 1650—only one hundred years after the Reformation, and when its influence had scarcely begun to be felt in these outlying districts—no vocations to the priesthood were forthcoming, even in so Catholic a district as Glengarry. One cannot but wonder, if this was due to the martial spirit which pervaded the Clans: how did they obtain vocations previous to the Reformation, when that spirit was surely equally strong?

In 1668 the Prefect of the Mission, Mr Alexander Winster, writes to the agent in Rome: "I sent five youths this year to our College in Paris, of whom three have already received the tonsure, and are studying Philosophy. But in the Highlands matters are quite different, for during all these years, of those educated in our school in Glengarry, we could not persuade one single youth to go abroad to study. This is due to the opposition of the parents, for I have tried my best. Of the necessity of procuring some youths, I was fully persuaded myself, and I was further urged thereto by the Superior of the said College at Paris, and by Mr William Leslie, our Procurator in Rome. The parents however consider their children sufficiently educated, when they have learned the first elements of grammar. They then take them away from school, and have resisted all the attempts of Mr Francis White and myself. Still I have great hopes of better success in the future, when they will have become a little more refined (*aliqualiter mitiores*) by education and religion."

Elsewhere in the same Report it is stated : " In some parts of the Highlands schools with Catholic teachers are tolerated, under the protection of the pious and influential Lord Macdonald. Still it will not be easy to find teachers in future, for, with the exception of Ewen M'Alaister—who has an allowance from Lord Macdonald —who would be willing to stay in a district so wild and so uncultivated ? He could expect nothing from his pupils, and would therefore need some attraction in the shape of a handsome salary. Certainly thirty scudi per annum would not be sufficient."

In 1677 the Prefect of the Mission reports : " There are two schools in the Highlands, the masters of which receive the same stipend as the Missionaries ; but so far are they from receiving anything from the parents, that these are hardly able to support their children when absent from their own homes. This arises from the fact that all their substance consists in flocks which afford them meat and dairy produce for food, and wool for clothing. One master, Ewen M'Alaister, who is married, has been teaching for many years. Another has just left because he could not stand the hard life. The two schools are under Mr Francis White."

In 1678, according to Mr Thomson, who for many years was agent in Rome, and left Notes for a History of the Church in Scotland, the school was transferred from Glengarry to Barra. No doubt the increased vigilance of the military made the former district unsafe, for about this period Government soldiers were actually quartered in Invergarry Castle.

Closely connected with the subject of vocations from amongst the Highland youths is that of the Irish priests, who at the urgent request of the Superiors of the Mission, and also of such lairds as Lord Macdonell, Clanranald, and M'Neill, of Barra, came over to give their services to the Catholics of the Highlands and Western Islands. Fathers White and Dugan have already been mentioned. Mr Hugh Ryan came to Scotland in 1680; in 1688 he was in Strathglass; in 1696 he was taken prisoner, and died in the November of that year.

Father Francis Macdonell, Franciscan, came to the Mission in 1668; in 1671 he sent his report on the Highland Mission to the Archbishop of Armagh, who transmitted it to Rome. In 1677 Father Macdonell was still in the Highlands. Father Peter Mulligan, an Augustinian, was brought from Rome by Bishop

Gordon, and they arrived together in Aberdeen in July, 1706. In 1722 Bishop Gordon writes to Rome: " Mr Mulligan has left us after sixteen years in the Highlands. He wished to serve his own countrymen, and during the many years he has been on the Mission he has reaped most abundant fruit of his labours, having reconciled over 700 persons to the Church."

Father Peter Gordon, Recollect, also served sixteen years on the Highland Mission, and left it in 1722 " at the command of his Superiors, who advanced him to a post of dignity in the Order." Many other Franciscans accepted the invitation of the Superiors of the Mission, but as they were largely under their own Superiors they do not appear on the annual lists of clergy. For Father Anthony Kelly, Bishop Hugh Macdonald had a special regard. He had been recalled by his Superiors, but Bishop Hugh made every endeavour to get him back. " If poor Anthony Kelly should come I would willingly dispense with all the rest." And in his letter to Propaganda he calls him " a most worthy and truly Apostolic man, who was on this Mission for many years, and did an immense amount of good." [1]

To return to the series of priests who attended the Glengarry district, Mr Robert Munro, mentioned in the foregoing Report as the indispensable companion of the visitor, was another of those wonderful men whom no adversity could conquer. He was three times imprisoned,

[1] Mr Thomson in his Notes states : " 1681. Mr James Devoyer and John Cahassy, two Irish priests, were persuaded to go to the Scots Mission for 3 years : they found only two priests in the Highlands. In 1687 Mr Haggarty, Irishman, and Mr Macdonald, a native, joined them. He was the first native Missioner, and unfortunately died after only six months "

and sentenced to death if he again returned from his banishment; but on each occasion he at once came back to his field of labour. In 1704, whilst lying prostrate with fever in a miserable hut in Glengarry, he was discovered by some English soldiers, who carried him off to the Castle, where he was thrown into the dungeon, and where, after receiving the vilest treatment, he was allowed to perish. He had been thirty-four years on the Highland Mission, and during the greater part of that time his principal residence was Glengarry and its neighbourhood.

Father M'Gregor, a Benedictine, was priest in Glengarry in 1728. He had come to Scotland in 1724, but only remained till 1730. Father William Grant, also a Benedictine, was in Glengarry in 1734, whilst in 1735 Mr Peter Grant had this Mission, but he too was here only two years, when he was sent as agent to Rome. Mr James Leslie followed, and he was still here in 1741. After him came Mr Æneas M'Gillis, who accompanied the expedition of Prince Charles Edward Stuart, as chaplain to the Glengarry men. These numbered over 600, under the command of Lochgarry. The chaplains with the Stuart army all wore the Highland dress, with sword and pistols, and went under the name of Captain.

It is a strange coincidence that Prince Charlie slept at Invergarry on 26th August 1745, one of the first days of his campaign, and returned there two nights after the fatal battle of Culloden. On the devastation wrought in the district after that most unfortunate undertaking there is no need to dwell. Situated as it was, midway between the hostile garrisons of Fort Augustus, Fort William and

Bernera, it suffered even greater barbarities than any other district.

Mr Æneas M'Gillis returned again to Glengarry, and was priest there from 1759 to 1767, when he reckoned that he had 1,500 Catholics under his care. He also at this period had the ministration of Lochaber with its 3,000 Catholics ; at first on account of the great age of Mr John Macdonald, and later on the death of this most holy priest, until a new appointment was made. In 1763 Abbate Grant, the agent in Rome, described Mr M'Gillis, in his Report, as a " learned, prudent and devout man who had studied at the Scots College, Rome, and is now about 40 years of age." Mr George Duncan " passed the remainder of his days at Glengarry, where he died on 13th March 1773, and is buried in St Finnans '' (Gordon).

In 1775 the Bishops reported to Rome that Alexander Macdonald and Roderick Macdonald had just arrived on the Mission. One had been placed in Uist, and the other (Mr Roderick) in Glengarry, in place of Mr Æneas M'Gillis, who was entirely invalided by gravel. In the previous year the Bishops had greatly praised Mr M'Gillis : " He had often served several missions at one time, and these most difficult ones by reason of their size and the number of their Catholics. He suffers so much from gravel that it is only with great pain that he can do any work. If he is called to attend the dying, as not rarely happens, he never refuses, but he is prostrate for several days afterwards." Mr M'Gillis died in 1777, when the Annual Report states : " For thirty-five years he had laboured with great zeal, and had given great satisfaction."

About this period Bishop Hugh Macdonald resided at Abercalder on the Eastern boundary of Glengarry.

He gave such assistance as he could, having chosen this district on purpose to be able still to do something in his old age. He died at Abercalder, 12th March 1773, and was buried at Kilfinnan, in Glengarry. Bishop Macdonald seems at one time to have intended making Glengarry his principal residence throughout his episcopate, even as it had been that of Mr White and Mr Munro. His first letter to Rome is certainly dated from " Lagani in Glengaria 13 Kal. Aprilis 1732."

The hope expressed by the prefect of the Mission in 1668, that vocations to the priesthood would soon come from the Highlands, was at this time amply fulfilled. Although the number of priests in the Highland district never came up to the needs of the people, as the letters of the Bishops clearly show, still the supply was fairly adequate. Of these the clan Macdonald supplied a remarkable majority, often to the great confusion of the authorities in Rome, since in 1777 there were no less than four Alexander Macdonalds out of the twelve priests. The lists for 1786 and 1794 are interesting in this connection, and go to prove that Austin Macdonald was not far wrong in writing to Propaganda: "The priests in the Highland District will soon be all Macdonalds."

Priests in the Highland District in 1786:

Samalaman	Bishop Alexander Macdonald Allan Macdonald
Lochaber	Angus M'Gillis
Glengarry	Ranald Macdonald
Moydart	Austin M'Donald
Arisaig	Alexander Macdonald Norman Macdonald

M

Knoydart   .   .   Alexander Macdonald
Morar   .   .   Ranald Macdonald

Priests in the Highland District in 1794:

Samalaman .   .   Bishop John Chisholm
Lochaber   .   .   Angus M'Gillis
Glengarry   .   .   Ranald Macdonald
Kintail   .   .   Christopher M'Rae
Arisaig   .   .   John Macdonald
Moydart   .   .   Norman Macdonald
Morar   .   .   Ranald Macdonald
Knoydart   .   .   Austin Macdonald
Lesser Isles .   .   Anthony Macdonald
Barra .   .   .   Allan Macdonald
Uist   .   .   . { Alexander Macdonald
                          { Ranald Maceachan

One other list may be inserted here. It shows how at this period the Scots College, Rome, was almost the sole source of priests for the Highland District.

Nomen			*Ordinatus*
Hugo MacDonald, Scalan .	.	.	1726
Æneas MacLauchlin, Parisiis	.	.	1712
Joannes Macdonald, Roma	.	.	1720
Alanus Macdonald, Roma .	.	.	1723
Nilus MacFie, Roma . .	.	.	1727
Æneas MacGillis, Roma .	.	.	1741
Alexander Macdonald, Roma	.	.	1746
Æneas Macdonald, Roma .	.	.	1752
Jacobus Leslie, Roma . .	.	.	1729
Alexander Forester, Roma .	.	.	1732

Jacobus Grant, Roma	1735
Petrus Grant, Roma	1735
Gulielmus Harrison (Henderson), Roma	1737
Joannes Macdonald, Roma . . .	1753
Alexander Macdonald, Roma . .	1753

Mr Roderick Macdonald remained in Glengarry until 1783, when he went to Canada. He had taken the Mission oath with the express stipulation that he should be free to go to America, whither all his relations had already preceded him.

It will not be out of place to give here some account of the new Glengarry in Canada, where many of the families of distinction found a home, and where Greenfield, Scotus, Abercalder, Leek and other names familiar in the history of Glengarry are perpetuated in that of the daughter colony. The first settlement was in Prince Edward Island, then called St John's Island, but this not proving very successful, many of the emigrants moved to the mainland of Nova Scotia, where the present county of Antigonish has many inhabitants whose forefathers came from Glengarry. By far the largest emigration, however, was that which followed Father Alexander MacDonell, after the disbandment of the Glengarry Fencible Regiment, about which a word must be said.

Father Alexander MacDonell, who proved so great a benefactor to his fellow-clansmen, was born in Glen Urquhart, Inverness-shire, about the year 1760. He probably spent some years at the school of Buorblach, near Loch Morar, then under the care of Bishop John Macdonald. The greater part of his student life was passed at the Scots College, Valladolid, which he entered in 1778, and where he was ordained in 1787. His first parish was that of Badenoch, and here he remained till 1792. He then went to Glasgow in charge of the Highlanders, who had been evicted from their holdings and had accepted the offer of the leading Glasgow merchants to settle in that city. To them Father MacDonell was everything—their priest, father, lawyer and protector.

But the trade of Glasgow declined rapidly at the outbreak of war between France and England, consequent on the French Revolution, and the Highlanders lost their employment and their means of livelihood. Father MacDonell then conceived the idea of utilising them by forming a Catholic regiment. In 1794 a meeting for this purpose was held at Fort Augustus, at which Mr Maxwell, of Terregles, presided. It was attended by Bishop John Chisholm, the Chief of Glengarry, Mr Fletcher of Dunans, Father MacDonell, and many others. The meeting unanimously resolved that a Catholic regiment be formed, with a Catholic commander and Catholic chaplain. The uniform was a close-fitting scarlet jacket, kilt and plaid of MacDonell tartan—dark green, blue and red. The officers had each the broad-bladed, basket-hilted claymore, and a dirk (skean-dhu), in addition to the long Highland pistols.

The regiment numbered over 800 men, half of whom came from the neighbourhood of Glengarry, and they were described at their first parade as " a most handsome body of men." That undoubtedly they were. The following is the list of officers :—

Colonel—Alexander Macdonell of Glengarry.

Lieut.-Colonel—Charles MacLean.

Major—Alexander Macdonald.

Captains—

Archibald M'Lachlan	James MacDonald
Donald MacDonald	Archibald Macdonell
Ronald Macdonell	Roderick MacDonald

Hugh Beaton

Capt.-Lieut.—Alexander Macdonell.

Lieutenants—

John MacDonald	James M'Nab
Ronald MacDonald	D. M'Intyre
Archibald M'Lellan	Donald Chisholm
James Macdonell	Allan M'Nab

Ensigns—

Alexander Macdonell	Donald MacLean
John MacDonald	Archibald Macdonell
Charles MacDonald	Alexander Macdonell
Donald Macdonell	Andrew Macdonell

Francis Livingstone

Adjutant—Donald Macdonell.

Quarter-Master—Alexander Macdonell.

Surgeon—Alexander Macdonell.

Chaplain—Rev. Alexander Macdonell.

The regiment at once gained the good will of the War Office by volunteering for service anywhere in Great Britain or the Channel Islands. They were accordingly sent to Guernsey in 1795, where they remained till 1798. They were then removed to Ireland, and here they saw the rest of their period of service, being disbanded after the Peace of Amiens in 1802, along with most of the other Fencible regiments. Father MacDonell had followed the regiment to Guernsey and to Ireland, and was now sorely perplexed what to do with the good fellows. After many difficulties he, in 1803, literally extracted from the

Government " a grant of land under the sign manual of the King " for every officer and soldier of the late Glengarry regiment, whom he might induce to settle in Upper Canada. Thus was formed the county of Glengarry, Ontario, which in 1848 numbered 15,000 inhabitants, and in 1900 over 50,000.

Father MacDonell remained still with the emigrants, who on more than one occasion showed their loyalty to the British Government. In 1812 the Glengarry Light Infantry Regiment was raised mainly through his exertions. They took part in no fewer than fourteen engagements, and on all occasions where fighting had to be done " Maighster Alastair " was at hand to see that it was well done. In 1819 he became Vicar Apostolic of the newly created district of Upper Canada, and, in 1826, Bishop of Kingston. He died in 1840, at Dumfries, whilst on a visit to Britain in connection with his emigration projects.

At the time of the raising of the Glengarry Fencibles, in 1794, Bishop Hay wrote : " I am much edified with Glengarry. He is an amiable young gentleman, and I hope will one day be an honour and support to his country and to religion." He certainly maintained the character of the " last of the Chiefs," appearing at Holyrood Palace with his " tail " of retainers, which surprised George IV. by its extravagance. He was intimate with Sir Walter Scott, whose Fergus MacIvor, in " Waverley," is none other than the Chief of Glengarry. He was drowned in the sinking of the *Stirling Castle*, in 1828, when his son, a youth of twenty, succeeded. But the extravagances of the late Chief and of his predecessors had so encumbered the estates that they had to be sold, and for many years now the chiefs of Glengarry have owned no portion of the glen of their fathers.

To return again to the series of priests. Mr Lamont was in Glengarry about 1815, and died there in 1820. Mr Donald Forbes, the veteran of Lochaber, spent the first years of his life as a priest in Glengarry (1819–1826). Bishop Ranald Macdonald, in his Report for 1822, says that the Catholics of Glengarry then numbered 800, under Mr Donald Forbes, a young priest of great piety, but delicate health, an Alumnus of Samalaman. He also had charge of 200 Catholics in Glenmoriston, and of 80 in Stratherrick. In view of the fact that Mr Forbes was priest in Lochaber for the almost unprecedented period of fifty-two years, the remark about his delicate health is certainly interesting.

The chapel at this time was at Newton, Abercalder, midway between Glengarry and Fort Augustus, where the foundations may still be seen. There would often be 500 people in church here. The altar was against the south wall, in the centre of it, and there was one entrance for the Kilchumin or Fort Augustus people at the east end of the building, and another for the Glengarry folk at the west end. Half-a-mile distant, just below the bridge over the Abercalder Burn, is the site of the house where Bishop Macdonald died.

The Ettrick Shepherd, James Hogg, visited Glengarry in 1803, and recorded his impressions. " On reaching Glengarry, the first place we came to was Greenfield, possessed by Mrs Macdonald. The house was really a curiosity. It was built of earth, and the walls were all covered with a fine verdure, but on calling we were conducted into a cleanly and neat-looking room, having a chimney, and the walls being plastered. The ladies, Mrs Macdonald and her sister, were handsome and genteelly dressed although unapprised of our arrival, unless by second sight. They were very easy and agreeable in their manners and very unlike the outside of their habitation. The family are Roman Catholics, and kept a young priest among them, but he had lately been obliged to abscond for some misdemeanour in marrying a couple secretly. He was much lamented by the whole family."

The Macdonalds of Greenfield had been amongst the largest tacksmen in Glengarry, but at the time the above letter was written they were holding prominent positions in Canada. The first large emigration, of which mention has already been made, was in 1773, for in the following year the Bishops reported that " the prosperous settlement of emigrants from South Uist under Glenaladale encouraged a large emigration from Glengarry, consisting chiefly of Catholics to the number of 300, including most of the leading country gentlemen. They sailed for New York in the autumn of 1773, attended by Mr M'Kenna, Missionary priest in Braelochaber."

Ten years later, in his Report to Propaganda of September, 1783, Bishop Alexander Macdonald states: " From the coast, if we proceed South, we come to the district of Glengarry, about 30 miles distant from the preceding. The intervening country is so wild, that it is only fit for grazing sheep in summer time. Glengarry is 18 miles long and six broad; a valley runs through the centre, enclosed by high hills. There is a military Fort here, with a village adjoining, in which are many non-Catholics, but the whole of the rest of the district is Catholic; the number of whom is 1,640, though some of

these are dispersed amongst the neighbouring districts.
To attend the whole number, at least two Missionaries
would be necessary, but they only have one, Mr Roderick
Macdonell, a good priest, educated at Douai."

Writing again in 1786; to the agent in Rome; Bishop
Alexander says : " Our Highland Catholics leave us in
great colonies : the hardships they suffer under their
squeezing and unfeeling masters, oblige them to look for an
asylum in distant regions. Last year upwards of 300 souls
left Glengarry and its neighbourhood, almost all Roman
Catholics, and settled in Canada above Mont Real where
were already settled about 800 Highlanders, who had
emigrated to America before the commencement of last
war, and are doing exceedingly well. To serve those
people, and because many of his own relations were
of the number, Mr Roderick MacDonald, an excellent
Missioner, went to America likewise."

Thirty years later Dr Macdonald, of Taunton, received
an interesting account of the Glengarry emigrants from
his friend, Mr D. M'Pherson. I give it almost in full,
as it occurs in " Memoir of Macdonald, of Keppoch."

"CHAMBLY, CANADA, N.A., 26th Dec. 1814.

" MY DEAR SIR,—Having just returned from a visit
of a month to the new county of Glengarry, I cannot help
endeavouring to give you some account of it, as well as
of the present condition of many of our countrymen who
were driven from their native land, and who directed
their course to America in search of better fortune.

" The county is a square of 24 miles, all of which and
the greater part of the next county (Stormont) are
occupied by Highlanders, containing at this moment from

1,100 to 1,200 families, two thirds of them Macdonalds. More able fellows of that name could be mustered there in twenty-four hours, than Keppoch and Glengarry could have done at any time in the Mother country.

" You might travel over the whole of the county and by far the greater part of Stormont, without hearing a word spoken but the good Gaelic. Every family, even of the lowest order, has a landed property of 200 acres ; the average value of which, in its present state of cultivation, with the cattle, etc., upon it may be estimated at from £800 to £1,000. However poor the family (but indeed there are none can be called so) they kill a bullock for the winter consumption ; the farm or estate supplies them with abundance of butter, cheese, etc., etc. Their houses are small but comfortable, having a ground floor and garret, with a regular chimney and glass windows.

" The appearance of the people is at all times respectable, but I was delighted at seeing them at church on a Sunday : the men clothed in good English cloth, and many of the women wore the Highland plaid. . . .

" The chief object of my visit to Glengarry was to see an old acquaintance, Mr Alexander Macdonald, a priest, who has been resident in this country ten years. I believe you know him, or at least you know who he is. A more worthy man is not in Canada ; he is the mainstay of the Highlanders here ; they apply to him for redress in all their grievances, and an able and willing advocate they find him. He is well known from the poorest man to the Governor, and highly respected by all. Were he ambitious of enriching himself, he might ere now be possessed of immense property ; but this appears not to be his object ; his whole attention is devoted to the good of the settlement; and the great and numerous services which he has done, cannot well be calculated.

"Colonel John Macdonald, of Aberhalder, died some years ago, and left one son and three daughters. . . . The Colonel's sister, Mrs Wilkinson, died a few months since, and left a son and three daughters—Mr Macdonald of Greenfield, who was married to the other sister, has a very considerable property here; he is Lieut.-Colonel of the Second Regiment of Glengarry Militia. One of his sons, Donald, is also Lieut.-Colonel; his second son is a Captain in the same corps . . . Mr Macdonald of Lundi died in this Settlement some time since, but his brother, Allan, now upwards of ninety, is still alive and well. . . . George Macdonald, son of Captain John Macdonald of Lulu, who died Captain of Invalids, at Berwick, recruited the Glengarry Regiment of Light Infantry, and is now Lieut.-Colonel commanding in this district, and Inspecting Field Officer of Militia. The good conduct of the Glengarry Light Infantry, as well as the Militia Regiments of the county, has been so frequently noticed and thanked in public orders, that it is unnecessary for me to say anything in their praise. They have on every occasion, when placed before the enemy, supported the character of Highlanders."

The emigrations of 1773, and of subsequent years, left but few of the older families in Glengarry; and at the present time there is only too much truth in the lines of W. Allan (*Celtic Mag.*, Oct., 1885):

" The Glen of my fathers no longer is ours,
    The Castle is silent and roofless its towers,
 The hamlets have vanished and grass growing green
    Now covers the hillocks where once they had been;

The song of the stream rises sadly in vain,
    No children are here to rejoice in the strain.
No voices are heard by Loch Oich's lone shore,
    Glengarry is here; but Glengarry no more "

Moreover it happened in Glengarry, as is so often stated
with regret by the Bishops in their Annual Letters, that
the families of substance emigrated, and left behind few
but those, whose circumstances did not permit of their
following. Time after time the Bishops complain of the
poverty of the priests at this period, so that we cannot be
surprised to find Mr Donald Macdonald, who was priest
in Glengarry from 1826 to 1835, inserting the following
appeal in the Directory for the latter year :—" The
Catholics of Glengarry are in great distress for want of
a suitable chapel. Some exertion must be made in order
to provide a decent place of worship for this large though
poor Congregation. Applications are now being made
for a site on which to build. As soon as one can be
procured, the incumbent will be under the necessity of
soliciting aid from the charitable on behalf of his flock,
which for all their covering, may be said at present to
worship their God on Sundays, and to assist at the Holy
Mysteries, in the open air."

In 1832 he wrote : " At present the place of worship
is a most miserable hovel, incapable of defending the
people, when assembled, from the inclemency of the
weather. It is in so ruinous a state that it can scarcely
be used with safety. To this may be added, that the
clergyman has no house of his own, and is under the
necessity of living with such families as are willing and
able to receive him."

Mr Macdonald was succeeded by Mr Donald Walker,
who remained till 1841, when he was in turn succeeded

by Mr Alexander Gillis. Mr Gillis built the church and presbytery, which were in use till 1883, and are now incorporated in the convent of Benedictine nuns. Though the chapel was thus moved three miles further from Glengarry, the good people still continued to attend it with striking regularity; whilst those living in the distant portions of Glenquoich were known to come the thirty miles to Fort Augustus, starting at four o'clock in the morning. Indeed it is noticeable that in the early directories Glenquoich is mentioned as served occasionally from Fort Augustus, but no mention is made of Glengarry, as though the seven miles were no objection to its being considered as part of the one parish. In 1888, however, the Benedictine Fathers at Fort Augustus began to say Mass in Glengarry itself, and in 1891 a small chapel was built at Mandally, where Mass is said every second Sunday. On the greater festivals, however, and especially at Christmas, the people of Glengarry still attend the church at Fort Augustus.

Mr Alexander Gillis was succeeded by Mr Valentine Chisholm (1842–1852), Mr Donald Mackenzie (1854–1860), Mr John Macdonald (1860–1871), Father Coll Macdonald (1871–1883), when the venerable Mission of Glengarry and Fort Augustus was taken over by the Benedictine Fathers.

The late Prior Vaughan was a man of great enthusiasms, and also of great ideals, and the circular which he issued at the time of the building of the Monastery of Fort Augustus forms interesting reading now, after a period of nearly forty years. "The Benedictine Order," he wrote, "is about to return to Scotland after an exile of some three hundred years, and the Monks of the

Benedictine Congregation have accepted the large quadrangular buildings of Fort Augustus, Inverness-shire, offered them by Lord Lovat.

" The Fort was built to accommodate a garrison of between two and three hundred soldiers, and has fallen into disuse as a military station since the Crimean War. Dr Johnson, who visited the Fort in 1773, says of it that ' the situation was well chosen for pleasure, if not for strength.' It is indeed eminently beautiful, commanding towards the East the long picturesque stretch of Loch Ness, and to the West, the grand rugged range of the Glengarry mountains. The Fort was erected in 1729 to overawe and subdue the Highlanders; and the Duke of Cumberland, who established his headquarters there after the Battle of Culloden, used to send forth parties to disarm and desolate the country, who did their work so ruthlessly as soon to cause the place to be held in general execration. . . . The Fort was purchased from the Government by the late Lord Lovat as recently as 1867, with a devout hope of his being able some day to find a religious order who would venture to establish themselves therein.

" The pious desire of the late Lord Lovat will now be fulfilled. Not only will this spot—once the scourge and terror of the Highlanders—become the source of many spiritual, and even temporal blessings to the surrounding neighbourhood, but here also the old English Monastery of Lamspring, and the Scotch College of Benedictines, which formerly existed at Ratisbon, will be restored, and the old Scottish line of Monks perpetuated. Of these there is still one venerable father surviving, destined to be the connecting link between the

FORT AUGUSTUS IN 1746

To face page 190

Monks of the past and those of the future, and whose
life appears to have been preserved thus far, that he
may at length see the day he has desired and prayed for
so long. Dunfermline and Melrose, Coldingham and
Arbroath, Paisley and Dundrennan, Kelso and Iona,
with some twenty other Abbeys observing the rule of
St Benedict, will live again, and the old chants which
have been silent for so many years, will be heard once
more in the land. How great and wide an influence the
new monastery is destined to exercise over the people of
Scotland we cannot venture to predict."

Whether the Abbey of Fort Augustus has realised all
these hopes it is not for me to say. I cannot but feel,
however, that if the good bishops and priests of old, who
had such an uphill struggle in their day, were to be asked
for their opinion, they would look with as great pleasure
and pride on the work being accomplished to-day, as we
look with admiration on the work which they accomplished. To the men of their day and to themselves,
they seemed to be doing little ; to us, who look at it from
a distance, their achievements were great and lasting.
May it be so likewise with the work of the present
generation, and of the Abbey of which so much was
hoped by its founders.

THE LESSER ISLES AND OTHER DISTRICTS

THE LESSER ISLES

In 1652 Father Dugan reported that he had visited the isles of Eigg and Canna, and had reconciled over 900 persons to the Church. A little later Father Francis MacDonell, in 1671, states: " There are other islands belonging to Clanranald, namely Canna, Rum, Eigg, and Muck, in which there are not less than 1,000 souls, all Catholics."

Bishop Nicolson and his companions sailed from Arisaig to Eigg on 18th June 1700. The wind was not in their favour, but by using their oars they reached the Isle of Eigg towards the middle of the day, having started at two o'clock in the morning. " This is a small island," his Report states, " which yields a fair quantity of grain and has excellent pasturage, though it is only three miles long. Of the inhabitants, all of whom are Catholics, 140 were confirmed. The houses of this, and indeed of all the other islands, are not constructed of wood, like those of the mainland (for in the Isles there is no wood except what is imported), but the walls are extremely thick. The two faces of the wall are of stone and the space between is filled in with earth in the manner of an embankment or rampart against the cold winds which blow from the ocean in winter. By order of the Chief of Clanranald we

192

were treated with great civility by his factor or deputy, a very intelligent man."

This Report next describes the atrocities committed by the captain of a man-of-war named Porringer, who had been sent to the Isles to harry the coast, and draw the men from following the royal army. This recalls to mind the terrible fate that befell the inhabitants of the island some years before, when they were almost all suffocated in the cave, at the narrow mouth of which their enemies, the Macleods, had kindled large fires. The floor of the cave is still strewn with the bones of the murdered inhabitants.

From Eigg Bishop Nicolson and his party passed on to Canna. This is described as a small island five miles in circumference, very fertile for its size and with abundance of pasturage, whilst the harbour on the south-east afforded safe anchorage. "At the entrance to this harbour there is a very high rock, in which it is thought there must be a mine of iron or adamant, since as the ships pass under it the compass turns towards the rock." One hundred and fifty years later this same rock is thus described: "In the vicinity of the harbour is an eminence called Compass Hill, which is said to disarrange the compass so much as to cause it to whirl round, so that when placed near it no faith can be put in its magnetic value."

The inhabitants of Canna were found to be all Catholics, and 100 were confirmed, partly on the outward journey and partly on the return from Uist. The priest at that time was Mr Hara, whilst Mr Morgan, as Dean, visited this and the neighbouring islands occasionally. The party left Canna at eleven o'clock in the evening, for the wind being favourable, and being near

N

midsummer, it was light all through the night. They had not gone far when a great calm came over the sea, so that they were surprised to find the water as smooth as glass, instead of the dangerous crossing they had feared.

In 1707 Bishop Gordon sailed from Arisaig for Uist, but the wind being again contrary, as it had been at the time of Bishop Nicolson's journey, he was carried to Eigg, where he spent two days On the return journey from Uist the Bishop visited Canna, where he gave Confirmation, but sailed again the same evening for Eigg.

The Report for 1763 states that the isles of Eigg and Canna used to have a priest to themselves, with about 400 Catholics, but they were at that time left destitute of any spiritual assistance except what the Bishop or his coadjutor could occasionally afford them. In 1767 the Abbate Grant reports that they still had no priest of their own, but the Report of 1777 states that the Lesser Isles were then under the charge of Mr Alan Macdonald, who had just returned from Spain, where he had taught for five years. In 1779 he voted in the election of Bishop Alexander MacDonald as " Alanus Macdonald, senior Missionarius in Insulis Minoribus."

In 1768 Mr Alexander Kennedy had been sent to Eigg, but he can only have been there a short time, for he died at Arisaig, in 1773. Abbé Macpherson says of him: " He came back to Scotland from Rome in 1767 and was ordained by Bishop John MacDonald. He gave great satisfaction as a Missionary in the Highlands, but lived only a few years thereafter, having died in 1773." One incident is noted in his missionary career. In 1770, when he landed on the small island of Muck, he was arrested by orders of Mrs Maclean, wife of the proprietor, who was then absent from home. He was taken to her house and kept in confinement for two days, until a boat could be procured to convey him back again to the mainland. None of his people were permitted to see him, and when he asked what offence he had committed, and offered every satisfaction, this lady's only reply was to cite the example of Boisdale, and announce her determination never to allow a priest again to set foot on her husband's estate. In the chapter on Uist it is shown how Boisdale later saw the folly of his persecution of the Catholics on his estate, and befriended both clergy and people. There is no record of Mrs Maclean following his example in this.

In 1783 the number of Catholics in Canna is given as 322, and in Eigg, 450, their priest at that time being Mr James M'Donald. In 1822 Bishop Ranald MacDonald writes: " Midway between the Outer Hebrides and the Mainland of Scotland are the Isles of Eigg, Rum and Canna, called the Lesser Isles, where there are 500 Catholics, of whom many emigrated this summer to America. The care of these is entrusted to Mr Anthony MacDonald who is often in great danger to health and life, especially in winter storms, which make the crossing from one island to another always a dangerous matter and often impossible. Mr Anthony is an Alumnus of Douai, is 53 years of age, and of delicate health. What I have said of the danger in sailing from one island to another applies to the priests who have care of all these islands." Mr Anthony MacDonald died in Eigg, 6th January 1843, in the forty-ninth year of his ministry and the seventy-third of his age. This latter detail we know from the letter of Bishop Ranald quoted above, although his age is omitted in the list of deceased clergy in the Directory of Scotland.

From 1834 till 1842 Mr Donald Mackay was priest in the Lesser Isles. This was his first parish, but he was to continue to labour for over fifty years in the High-lands. He had been born at Frobost, in South Uist, in 1804. In 1823 he entered the seminary of Lismore, and the following year was sent to Propaganda, where he had a most distinguished course, gaining numerous medals. He was ordained in 1833, and had charge of the Lesser Isles from 1834 to 1842. Thence he was sent to North Morar, where he remained twenty-nine years, during seventeen of which he had charge of Knoydart also. In 1871 he went to Drimnin, where he remained till his death in 1886. In the December of that year the illness from which he suffered took so serious a turn that the last rites of the Church were administered to him. His patience, resignation and childlike piety were all along truly edifying. He lingered for some days, comforted by the presence of his Bishop, who stayed with him for a week, and gave him Holy Communion daily. On the morning of 4th January he peacefully expired. His body, which was sent, at his own request, to his native place for burial, was conveyed by steamer to Loch Bois-dale, where it was received by the priests of Daliburg and Bornish, and interred in the Hallan Cemetery, Dali-burg. Mr Mackay was a man of sterling piety and exceptionally lively faith. In disposition he was kindly, affable and cheerful. He was reputed a good Hebrew scholar, spoke Latin with grace and fluency, and to the end wrote Italian remarkably well. He was a thorough master of Gaelic and a powerful preacher in the language (Directory, 1888). The varied accomplishments of this most worthy priest remind one of the saying of Bishop Nicolson that the Catholic Highlanders "were of very lively spirits and were wonderfully successful when they had a little education." The same has indeed been remarked time after time when students from the Highlands came in competition with others in the colleges abroad.

Another of the good old priests who had charge of the Mission of Eigg was Mr Alexander Gillis, who was there from 1842 till his death in 1889. He was born at Sunart, in Argyllshire, in 1806, and entered the college of Lismore in 1825. From there he went to Rome, where he was ordained in 1840. He was appointed to Fort Augustus, including Glengarry, where he laboured for three years with great zeal and success. He had just completed the building of a new church and presbytery when he was removed, in 1842, to the ancient and interesting mission—to use the words of the obituary notice —of the Lesser Isles. This embraces the islands of Eigg, Rum, Canna and Muck. The Catholic population at present is probably 250 souls, but at that time it was considerably more. The emigration of some of the best of his flock had a very depressing effect upon their pastor. From that date things, from a pecuniary point of view, went from bad to worse with him, till at last his house—especially the roof—became quite dilapidated. His robust constitution, instead of being injured by this dreadful exposure, seemed to rejoice in it. Most probably any three ordinary priests under the same circumstances would have broken down during the period of thirty-seven years, during which he manfully stood his ground. In winter his isolation was almost complete. Let us give an idea of this. Some twenty years ago, Arisaig was the post town for Eigg. One winter twelve consecutive *Tablets* (a weekly paper, of course) lay at the Arisaig post office for him, because a boat could not venture to cross the Sound all that time. Things are now changed: steam communication is frequent, and the chapel and house have been put in a thorough state of repair.

Eigg itself is a lovely spot, a truly picturesque island, and amazingly rich from a geological point of view. Mr Gillis was greatly attached to it. Bishop M'Kinnon, of Arechat, North America, offered him a good parish if he would go there, but he declined the generous offer. On another occasion Bishop Gray desired him to accept the mission of Iochar, South Uist, but he still clung to his island home He evidently wished to die in harness, and his desire was granted. He died in the most edifying manner, fortified by all the rites of the Church, and after having given throughout his life an example of extraordinary patience, under the most trying circumstances.

The priests of this Mission in more recent times have been Rev. Donald M'Lellan, 1883-1888; Rev. Donald Walker, 1889-1903; Rev. John Macneil, 1901-1906; Rev. John Macmillan, 1906-1909; Rev. Fred. M'Clymont, 1910-1914. The latter had the pleasure, in 1910, of opening a new church and presbytery, for which he had collected the necessary funds in various parts of Great Britain. For almost seventy years the Catholics of Eigg had used as a chapel the lower floor of an old farm-house, the rest of the building being used as a presbytery. Before that they were even worse off, while tradition has it that at one time Mass used to be said in a large cave, still known as the Cave of Devotion. With the erection of a new church and presbytery a happier condition of things has been started, and we may hope that the Catholics of Eigg and Canna will steadily increase, and will soon exceed in numbers those whom Bishop Nicolson and the early missionaries found there.

Regarding the different chapels, previous to 1810 the church and priest's house were at the south-east side of the island. The house was originally a small, two-storied building, though later the upper story was taken down. At present it is little more than a ruin, whilst the croft has been incorporated in Kildonan farm. The circumstances of the change from this older chapel to the one recently in use are thus described by Mr Donald Mackay : " My grandfather was fiddler to the Laird of Muck, and he had so great a reputation as a musician that Clanranald determined to have him on his own property. Said Clanranald to my grandfather : ' If you will settle in the Island of Eigg, I will give you a fine house and a good croft.' Well my grandfather went over and had a look at the house, but he was not pleased at all, at all! However it happened that the priest was wanting the big house, and my grandfather thought that the priest's house and croft would suit him well, so they exchanged, and that is how Mr Anthony came over to the West side of the island." This tale is interesting as showing the size of the chapels of that date, for though it may have been large as crofters' houses went, it could scarcely have had much accommodation for the 150 to 200 people who at that time came to their Sunday

Mass. The floor was merely the hard earth, on which clean sand was sprinkled previous to the Sunday service, and then those "who had a mind" would take with them a peat to kneel on. The lower floor of the house was the chapel, the rest of the building being used as a presbytery. Mr Gillis is still remembered for his skill at shinty. It has been the custom from time immemorial, among Catholics and Protestants alike, to play shinty every Christmas and New Year on the fine sandy beach of Laig Bay. The older generation still remember how Mr Gillis would join in the game, barefooted like the rest. They say that till the latter days of his life he was the nimblest of players.

In confirmation of what has been said of the difficulty in serving the Catholics in different islands, the tale is told how Mr Gillis had started for Canna one day, but, on account of the bad weather, his boat had to put back. On landing he met the Minister, Mr Sinclair, with whom he was on very good terms. Next day he started off again, and again he had to put back. As he landed there was the Minister again at the landing-place, ready to condole with him, but really to chaff him on his bad luck. It actually happened, that on the third attempt Mr Gillis only got as far as Rum, when he had to return without being able to get to Canna. This time he took every precaution to avoid the Minister, and thought he had succeeded in doing so. But no; just as he reached his house, Mr Sinclair passed from the opposite direction, and both of them laughed heartily at the incident.

Canna, like its sister isle, is very interesting, historically and geologically. There are the remains of old Columban cells at the foot of a steep cliff, called Scur na

Ban naomh. The island before the Reformation always had a close connection with Iona, and for a long time it was the property of the monks, being most probably the Eilean naomh, or Holy Island, of Adamnan.

The present Catholic Church stands on an eminence overlooking the entrance to the harbour. The little church is really very handsome, having a tower and a pretty porch all in correct Norman style. The church and tower are a good guide to sailors making for the harbour. It was built by the Dowager Marchioness of Bute, in memory of her father, Lord Howard of Glossop. Previously the Catholics had an unpretentious little building on the Canna side, which is now the post office. In spite of the difficulties in the way of the priest coming from Eigg to visit them, there seems to be a special Providence over the Canna people, for they never die without his aid at the end. This confidence of the people of Canna seems always to have distinguished them, for Mr Alexander Leslie bears witness to it as early as the year 1678. He says: "From Rum we visited another very beautiful island, Canna, where all the inhabitants are Catholics. They were filled with joy on seeing us, not having seen a priest for more than a year. Their spiritual necessities and their fervent zeal forced us to stay amongst them for a few days, all the more so that they had many children to be baptized. Some heretical preachers had indeed passed that way recently, and had offered to baptize the children, but the parents would not allow it. The preachers assured them that the priest would consider the baptism valid, but they would not have their children baptized by heretics, saying: 'God will send us a priest in His own good time.'"

GLENMORISTON

SITUATED as they were, midway between the two Catholic districts of Glengarry and Strathglass, the people in the upper end of Glenmoriston ever retained their ancient faith. In 1763 there were 200 Catholics in the glen; in 1783 Bishop Alexander MacDonald states that there were 160 Catholics under Mr Æneas M'Donald, who also had charge of the 200 recent converts in Kintail. In 1822 Bishop Ranald MacDonald mentions that the Catholics of Glenmoriston were then under Mr Donald Forbes, priest of Glengarry. The Directory of 1842 is the first which mentions Glenmoriston as a separate mission, the pretty little chapel and priest's house having been completed in the previous year. Mr Alexander Macdonald was then the priest there, but already, in 1846, Mr Angus Gillis had succeeded him. Mr Gillis also had charge of the Catholics in Stratherrick.

The following year the mission was vacant, and was attended by the priest from Strathglass. In 1849 Mr James Lamont was residing here; whilst in 1857 the services were given by the priest from Fort Augustus, the congregation being then stated to number about eighty souls. Thus the small numbers of the congregation have made it always uncertain whether there would be a resident priest there or not, whilst at the present time the numbers have still further decreased. The chapel, however, and the little priest's house—the latter so small that one wonders how the men of last century lived therein—are beautifully situated on the banks of the river Moriston, just below one of the most picturesque bridges in the whole of Scotland. It was built by Telford at the beginning of last century, when the road which here stretches right across Scotland was constructed.

If the beauties of Nature were sufficient to attract a population back to the land, then certainly Glenmoriston would soon be thickly populated. I have visited it hundreds of times, and have taken many visitors across the hill from Fort Augustus into Glenmoriston, always to hear the same delighted enthusiasm for the beautiful valley, which seems even more attractive now that the ruined cottages and deserted homesteads add a touch of sadness to the charming view. It is, moreover, full of memories of Prince Charlie and the Forty-five. Over 200 Grants of Glenmoriston met the prince at Abercalder, four miles west of Fort Augustus, on his victorious journey south ; whilst after the defeat of Culloden, nowhere was the prince more safe than amongst his devoted followers of Glenmoriston.

GLENCOE

THERE is little doubt but that the massacre which has rendered Glencoe so famous was very largely due to religious bigotry. It is so represented in the letters of the time to Propaganda. The Macdonalds of Glencoe were all Catholics ; they formed, indeed, the southernmost portion of the Catholic belt, which extended from Glencoe almost uninterruptedly to Knoydart They were thus the " buffer state " between the Catholic districts to the North and the non-Catholic to the South. They were also the southernmost portion of the Macdonalds, the inveterate enemies of the Campbells, to whom the massacre was entrusted.

The story has been too often told to need repetition here. Suffice it to say that forty unarmed men, women and children were massacred by troops, to whom they had extended most friendly hospitality, under the assurance that they should sustain not the least injury. There were 200 persons living in the Glen at the time, and all under seventy years of age were ordered to be destroyed. The stormy weather, however, delayed part of the soldiers who were to have taken part in the massacre, and thus 160 persons were known to have made their escape, though their sufferings amid the hills in that month of February were terrible to narrate.

The Catholics of Glencoe were in early days under the charge of the priests of Lochaber, but in 1836 a chapel was built in the Glen by Mr Charles Mackenzie, then priest at Fort William. The congregation numbered about 100, according to the Directory of that date. For many years now Glencoe has had a resident priest, whilst in 1909 another chapel was opened at Kinlochleven to accommodate the Catholics who were employed at the works there. At the present date, therefore, this old established Mission is more numerous than at any previous time in its history.

STRATHERRICK

THE earliest mention which I have found of Stratherrick among the papers at Propaganda is that of 1822, when Bishop Ranald Macdonald stated in his Report that there were eighty Catholics there, attended to by the priest of Glengarry. Later this congregation was served from Glenmoriston, until, in 1859, the present chapel and priest's house were built on land granted by Lord Lovat, whose properties extend for several miles on the south side of Loch Ness.

The number of Catholics in this mission was recently increased by the opening of large aluminium works at Foyers, five miles distant. With the establishment of these power stations—that at Kinlochleven belongs to the same company—with the settlement of crofters under the Small Holdings Act, and with the expected action of Government in planting large areas for afforestation, we may hope that the Highland districts will once again be thickly populated. May the Highland Catholics of the future often think of those mentioned in the foregoing pages, who strove so hard to keep the Light of the Old Faith burning, and who made such great sacrifices in its behalf.

NOTES

NOTE I

It will be remembered that Father Dugan had been educated at St Lazarre, Paris, where everything would doubtless be scrupulously neat and clean, and as well provided as the religious profession of the house would permit. On arriving in the Highlands, however, he was a proscribed person, and as such accepted shelter from any who offered it ; often, doubtless, his lot was amongst the very poorest, and it is to these that the remarks in his letter seem to apply. His statements are corroborated by Bishop Nicolson (*see* p. 122), who seems to infer that not only the clothing, but also the food, of the upper classes was much superior. It will be noted that Bishop Nicolson also had often to take shelter in the shielings, avoiding, probably, the main routes in order to travel the more unobserved.

NOTE II

The term " black house " is one frequently used in the Highlands even at the present time. The older cottages were roofed with heather or straw, and as this grew old it assumed a very dark colour, nearly black. The interior of the cottage was generally open right up to the

206

roof, the timbers of which became coloured by the peat smoke, so as almost to appear to have been covered with black varnish. This was especially the case when the peat fire was in the centre of the room, as was the almost invariable custom one hundred years ago.

NOTE III

The ruins of *Lovat Castle* may be traced on the banks of the Beauly river, close to the present farmhouse of Wester Lovat, and about three miles from Beaufort Castle, the more recent residence of the family. Part of the walls of the castle are now incorporated in the farm buildings, while the terraces cut in the bank of the river can distinctly be seen. At a short distance is an old pear-tree, which at one time formed part of the garden.

INDEX

O

PRINTED IN GREAT BRITAIN BY
THE RIVERSIDE PRESS LIMITED EDINBURGH

CPSIA information can be obtained
at www.ICGtesting.com
Printed in the USA
BVOW09s1454300118
506720BV00010B/298/P